AF538707

RE-ENGINEERING OF HUMAN RESOURCES

Edited by

Prof. Rabi N. Misra

Department of Management Studies
S.M.I.T. Biju Patnaik University
Berhampur (Orissa)

DISCOVERY PUBLISHING HOUSE PVT. LTD.

NEW DELHI-110 002

Published by:
Tilak Wasan
DISCOVERY PUBLISHING HOUSE PVT. LTD.
4383/4A, Ansari Road, Darya Ganj
New Delhi-110 002 (India)
Phone : +91-11-23279245, 43596064-65
Fax : +91-11-23253475
E-mail : parul.wasan@gmail.com
discoverypublishinghouse@gmail.com
web : www.discoverypublishinggroup.com

***First Edition:* 2012**

ISBN: 978-93-5056-019-8

Re-Engineering of Human Resources

Printed at:
Shree Balaji Art Press
Delhi

Preface

Re-engineering of Human Resources is an important business process of an organization. Human Resources function implements new policies regarding selection, appointment and training of staff in such a manner that the performance appraisal of the staff will reach to an optimum level. Re-engineering is a fundamental re-thinking and radical redesigning of business process to achieve dynamic improvement in cost, quality, price etc.

In present day context, human capital is considered most valuable and important with comparison to other assets of a business concern. Re-engineering of Human Resources in recent era will help for re-designing of business undertaking to meet the challenges of the global market.

Unless and until Human Resources management would given due importance, it will curtail the growth of the organization. The work audit will be given due importance than the financial audit of an organization. This book will be helpful to HR managers of business organization and to the management students of all universities.

Dr. R.N. Misra

Acknowledgements

I am thankful to all paper contributors for this book. It is not possible in my part to edit this book without their active co-operation and help.

My wife Smt. Swarna Prava Misra has taken all positive steps for editing this boo4k. My son Roopesh, Rookesh along with my daughter-in-law Amrita (Lecturer in English) were taken all the pain for editing this book.

I convey my thanks and express gratitude to Mr. Tilak Wasan, the Director/Owner of Discovery Publishing House Pvt. Ltd., New Delhi for publishing this book without any hesitation. His son Mr. Parul Wasan, and other members of the staff of Discovery Publishing House for their kind help and co-operation in publishing the book in time.

Dr. Rabi N. Misra

Contents

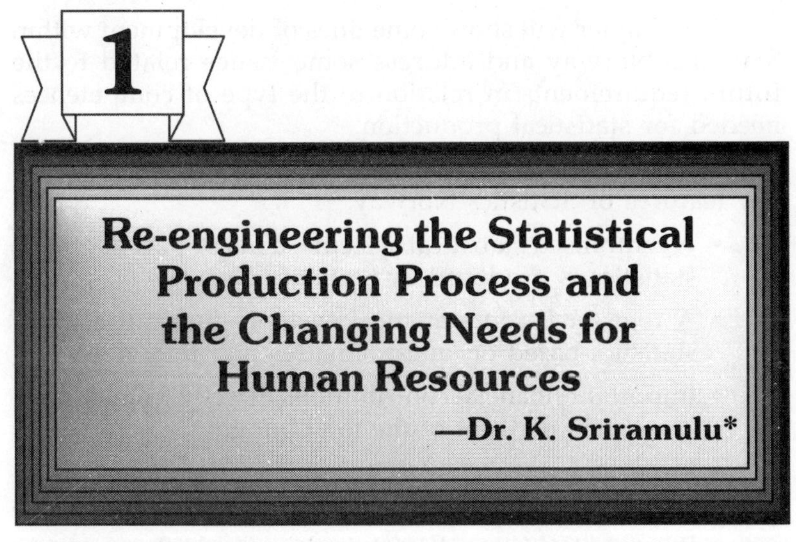

1 Re-engineering the Statistical Production Process and the Changing Needs for Human Resources

—Dr. K. Sriramulu*

Introduction

The volume and variety of official statistics produced in Norway has been developing rather fast over the last 30-35 years, linked to increased demand both at national and international level. This development has been made possible through growing resources to the production of official statistics. However, the increased accessibility to diverse numeric administrative sources and the technological development which facilitates the registration, checking and management of large data sets, have contributed substantially to this development. Thus the increasing volume of statistics can be produced and disseminated with a lower input of manual handling. This change in processes has also led to

---

* Reader in Commerce Govt. Degree College, Srikakulam, Andhra University A.P.

change's in the requirements for manpower and not least changes in required competences, and it is expected that this process will continue.

This chapter will show some lines of development within Statistics Norway and address some issues related to the future requirements in relation to the type of competences needed for statistical production.

As a background it is necessary to take into account some key features of Statistics Norway:

- A centralised statistical system—a major part of official statistics is produced by Statistics Norway
- A register-based statistical system—but still a lot of statistics-based on questionnaires and interviews
- Important financial contributions directly from users—around 30 per cent of the total budget
- Important research activity—one of the largest social science institutes in Norway with almost 100 researchers
- Present staff around 1000, with around 60 per cent in Oslo and 40 per cent in Kongsvinger (90 km from Oslo). No regional offices.

A look in the mirror

The expansion of statistical system of Norway especially in the 1970s and 1980s meant a considerable increase in staff for data entry, control and editing, especially in connection with the 1980 census.

During the 1980s Statistics Norway developed an internal training programme in order to provide systematic training of staff with no academic background (upper or lower secondary background). The recruitment of such staff, especially in Kongsvinger, was quite easy at that time. With targeted training this staff has been very stable and efficient in running the statistical production processes in many areas.

However, after the 1990 census operation there was an overcapacity of staff in the field of data registration and control. This overcapacity was increased through the gradual process of extending the use of administrative sources instead of direct data collection reading solutions. Thus a transformation programme was initiated. To make use of the capacity and the competences in the field of data entry Statistics Norway on a temporary basis took on some tasks related to massive data registration from other governmental bodies. At the same time, those who wanted, were given the support for additional internal or external training courses, or offered on the job training in a subject matter unit. In 1993 more than half the staff had non-academic background (secondary school or primary school, possibly supplemented with internal training.

The expansion of Statistics Norway in thc late 1990s mainly meant recruiting staff with higher academic education, which in 2000 counted 42 per cent of all staff. This expansion was strongly related to the integration of Norwegian statistics with the European Statistical System, which also meant more staff to analyse thc requirements, and to transform these requirements into new statistical production processes and products.

Thus also the systematic training program for non-academics was closed down and replaced by a series of training courses adapted on an annual basis to the needs of all staff.

The number of non-academics decreased slightly during the period 1993-2000.

After 2000 the expansion of Statistics Norway continued in response to new national and European requirements, by recruiting academics with higher and lower degree. At the same time the number of non-academics was reduced to around 25 per cent, mainly by replacing non-academics with staff with academic background.

The process was made possible by a more systematic use of administrative sources which was enabled by the new statistical legal act in 1989, and through implementation of new technologies related to data collection, data entry and data management. By the direct utilisation of administrative electronic files the resources used for data entry and data editing were reduced. Furthermore use of scanning and electronic questionnaires contributed to improved efficiency in this part of the production process. By analysing how available manpower resources (holiday and sick leaves excluded) are distributed among main areas of operation. It can be seen that resources going to production and compilation of statistics has been slightly decreasing from 2000 till 2007, but is still 49 per cent. On the other hand more resources are being used on development projects, raising to 12 per cent in 2007. This fact illustrates the increased focus on improved tools and methods to produce statistics more efficiently and with higher quality—which also affects the requirements for new types of competences.

The resources used on general support, including IT infrastructure has decreased, whereas somewhat more resources are used on research/analysis and administration.

It is worth noting that the study background of staff has become more and more diversified. Some years ago the majority of staff with master degree in the subject matter and research departments had a socio-economic study background (in 1991 around 50 per cent). Now around 27 per cent have a master degree in social sciences, which could mean different directions of specialisation such as economics, geography, sociology or political science. Another 22 per cent have a master degree in socio-economics. The rest has quite varied background, including for instance business economy, mathematics, engineering and agricultural economy.

Training in Statistics Norway

As the background of staff is becoming more and more varied it has been necessary to develop more targeted training. It is especially acknowledged that not all new staff get sufficient introduction to statistical methods and understanding during their studies. The internal training programme consisted of 96 courses in 2007 with around 1200 participants, using 18 000 hours on course attendance. About one half of the staff attended at least one course.

A major part of the resources went to the development programme which has two main branches; introductory courses for new staff and a programme for project and teamwork (Proteam). The introductory courses for new staff runs according to needs and covers altogether 8 days, of which 3 days are allocated to statistical methods. A redesign of this course is underway in order to target the course better to actual needs of new staff. The programme on project and teamwork runs over 8-9 months with four joint training courses and a total of 12 days. In addition, the participants are expected to work on a regular basis on the project which is chosen for the project work. The objective is to provide the participants with knowledge on project work, to develop competences for cooperation and team building and to introduce how Statistics Norway defines quality work.

A major part of the training is also allocated to IT competences. Several of the courses are rather practical, such as the use of powerpoint, a project planning tool or e-mail, whereas other courses are more IT specific such as use of Unix, SAS or Excel. In 2008 around 460 000 Euros are budgeted for different internal training courses. In order to motivate training and competence development of academic staff Statistics Norway has implemented a scheme for qualification to statistical adviser. This programme started with a pilot in 2002. The target group is employees who, have worked in Statistics Norway 5 years or more, having at least equivalent to bachelor degree academic background. The candidate should write a comprehensive application with CV describing various work tasks that includes work with international or national committees and programmes. The candidate should join written documentation such as articles, notes on plans and method as well as final publishing of statistics. The qualifications of the candidate are to be evaluated by a committee of appointed experts with relevant qualifications. The committee must include a minimum of four experts, and at least one must be statistical expert external to Statistics Norway, for instance from Sweden or Finland. The candidate is to be evaluated on the basis of the following documentation: Application and CV; Written documentation on work performed; Statements by the responsible manager.

The candidates are evaluated on the basis of formal qualifications, qualifications in statistical methods and qualifications in official statistics, but they should also document experiences from different fields of statistics and teamwork abilities. In the period 2002-2007 there were altogether 84 applicants of which 41 were judged as qualified for being statistical adviser. An evaluation considers that the qualification programme has to some extent reduced turnover and also contributed to improved quality of statistical production in several areas.

Thus also the degree of seniority is changing. In 2007 almost 40 per cent have worked more that 20 years at Statistics Norway, whereas this percentage in 1991 was below 20. It is interesting to note that the percentage with less than 5 years of service was at the same level in these two years, 29 and 26 per cent competences and production capacity in some areas. One reason for this turnover might be that new academics with a master degree are not satisfied with the job content, even if one also should take into account the general pressure of the Norwegian labour market, the wage level in the governmental sector and that the new generation is less stable in relation to the labour market.

Thus Statistics Norway faces several challenges to be addressed:

What will be the possibilities to recruit and keep well qualified staff—in both the two locations of a Oslo and Kongsvinger in future?

What are the effects of technological and methodological development in relation to required competences?

How to develop a more targeted training programme that takes into account the background of the staff and the new requirements?

How can we cooperate with external partners in order to ensure future recruitment with proper competences?

In 2007 Statistics Norway decided upon a strategy for human resource as a sub strategy of the overall strategy document 'Strategy 2007' (http://www.ssb.no/english/about_ssb/strategy/). The main headlines of this strategy are:

- Forward-looking and transparent management
- Sharing knowledge
- High-quality on-the-job training
- An attractive employer
- Expertise development—a joint responsibility

This strategy is being implemented through different concrete actions in the annual work programmes.

A programme for improving business processes

Statistics Norway started early 2008 a programme for improving and standardisation of the statistical production system ('FOSS'). The programme focuses on developments in the following areas:

- Development of standardised work processes, methods and IT systems
- Development of systematic quality measures and control
- Development of the organisation and competences within the organisation in accordance with the previous two areas. An action on competence development in relation to FOSS is going to start, and there are some

assumptions that will have to be analysed and studied further:

- The success of the whole programme will depend very much on available competences and capabilities, not least capabilities for reorientation and innovation and willingness to take on new tasks.
- The programme, if succeeded, will change the required competences; some technical and routine oriented tasks will be standardised/eliminated, whereas the need for more analytical and management competences will increase.
- The programme might change the needs for internal training, motivate for increased internal job rotation and also the specification of competences when recruiting new staff.
- Some projects examples within the FOSS programme:
- **Integrated system for estimation and editing (ISEE):** To develop and extend the usage of standardised methods for estimation and editing including a general IT solution
- **Common metadata base for input data (SMED):** To develop/adapt a user-friendly metadata base to be used for different data collection projects.
- **Coordination of samples for economic surveys (NorSamu):** To improve, standardise and coordinate the planning of samples and the sampling. These projects, as well as other projects, are assumed to have major impacts on the future needs for man power, competences required and on internal organisation. It is for instance assumed that due to standardisation across the organisation, staff can more easily change job. At the same time, increased internal rotation might be a requirement

in order to contribute to standardisation of working methods and to develop a common culture. It is further assumed that these projects will lead to less routine work, more challenging tasks and more time for analysis and follow up of users. It is also assumed that the fulfilment of the FOSS programme might affect the overall organisation. An increased focus on standardised business processes, linked to the business model shown below, might lead to new ways of thinking about the way different functions and tasks are distributed. To some extent Statistics Norway already has centralised some functions related to data collection in a department for IT and data collection. But there might be further changes as a result of the ongoing process. One issue is the degree of centralisation of IT, where there now are some IT units linked to some departments.

The main elements of the present organisation are:

Four subject matter departments

(*i*) Economics, energy and the environment (6 divisions, staff around 127)

(*ii*) Social statistics (5 divisions, including an IT division, staff around 137)

(*iii*) Industry statistics (5 divisions, including an IT division, staff around 162)

(*iv*) National accounts and financial statistics (5 divisions, including an IT division, staff around 127)

Research department (7 divisions, staff around 95)

Four horizontal departments

(*i*) Management support (2 divisions, staff around 47)

(*ii*) Administrative affairs (3 divisions, staff around 55)

(*iii*) Communication (3 divisions, staff around 55)

(*iv*) IT and data collection (6 divisions, staff 150)

Statistics Norway has thus a mixture of a subject matter oriented organisation and a functional organisation. Over the years there have been different trends in direction of centralisation/decentralisation. Centralisation has also been linked to functional specialisation. For the moment there might be a push in the direction of functional specialisation, partly as the result of the mentioned FOSS programme.

Towards a Framework for Competence Description

In order to be better plan future recruitment and training it has been considered useful to draft and discuss a framework for the description of different competences. In this process it has been very useful to learn from the examples and experiences from other countries. One interesting example is from Australian Bureau of Statistics (ABS) as presented in a document to the Conference of European Statisticians in 2006 (ECE/CES/2006/22). There it is differentiated between 'Core capabilities' and 'Job specific capabilities'. As *Core capabilities* are defined as those capabilities required of all employees in the ABS, regardless of role or business unit. These are generic capabilities and form the foundation for statistical excellence. As the main items of core capabilities are listed:

(*a*) People and Communication

(*b*) Achieving Results

(*c*) Thinking

(*d*) Understanding the Business of Statistics

(*e*) Understanding the ABS Environment

Job-specific capabilities are applied to specific roles, job groups and functions. Such capabilities are developed for Statistical and Methodological, Information Technology and Client and Corporate roles.

As the most critical set of Job-specific capabilities are considered the statistical capabilities which aligned to the Statistical Business Cycle are:

(*a*) Stakeholder Engagement

(*b*) Statistical Planning

(*c*) Methodology

(*d*) Collection Development

(*e*) Data Collection

(*f*) Processing

(*g*) Data Analysis

(*h*) Dissemination

(*i*) Decision Support

(*j*) Managing Quality and Processes

Other examples can be picked from documents from for instance Finland (ECE/CES/2006/14) or Sweden (ECE/CES/2006/30) presented at the same conference. The job-specific capabilities as defined by ABS can related to the business model as specified for the standardisation programme (FOSS) of Statistics Norway. This process model was originally developed by Statistics New Zealand and is implemented in some other NSIs and also proposed by the UNECE secretariat as the basis for a common generic model at a seminar in April 2008 (Working paper No. 10): 9 Statistics Norway will continue working on specifying a framework for competence description as a basis for improved training and follow up, and will benefit from any exchange of ideas concerning solutions and approaches.

Organisational Development and the Needs for Competences and Training

One challenge also in relation to training is that when combining this business model with the present organisational chart, we see that the different process steps can be located in different places in the organisation. A schematic organisational chart can in principle look like this: Thus one might imagine the following responsibilities in the different parts of the organisation: Function Subject matter unit; Functional support unit; Research unit—

1. Specifications of needs Main Partly?
2. Develop and design Main/partly Main/partly?
3. Build Main/partly? Main/partly?
4. Collect Main
5. Process Partly Main
6. Analyse Main Partly
7. Disseminate Main/partly Main/partly?
8. Quality management Main Partly Support and infrastructure Main

We see that there are some roles that will have to be clarified in this type of organisation, which also will affect both recruitment and internal training of staff. In this context it is worth noting some of the lessons learned in Statistics New Zealand when implementing a process-based approach (Working Paper No. 3, MSIS 2008). It is mentioned that there are several benefits, but that there are some side effects that have to be mitigated, for instance:

- Governance becomes more complex
- Increased challenge to find and retain skilled staff

Concluding Remarks

Human resource management is a major challenge in a statistical agency, especially in a situation of changing technologies, organisation and working processes. An issue is also to what extent the national education system can provide the educational background that is relevant for the tasks of modern statistical system, and how supplementary competences and capabilities might be provided. Increased cooperation between national statistical institutes in the area of training, exchange of best practises and exchange of staff can be an important answer to these challenges. Some issues for further consideration are:

- To what extent is there a common business model for statistical production?
- What are the relationship between this business model, the organisational set up and the requirements for human resources and the competences required?
- To what extent has this business model consequences for the competence structure, for instance in relation to degree of specialisation, required background and internal training?
    - ❖ To what extent can we share a common description of the required competences and capabilities of a statistical institute?
    - ❖ How can we benefit from benchmarking and sharing best practice in the field of human resource management and organisational development?
    - ❖ To what extent is it possible to develop an international labour market for experts in official statistics?

REFERENCES

Process-based IT Organization at Statistics New Zealand. Working paper No. 3, Joint UNECE/Eurostat/OECD meeting on Management of Statistical Information Systems (MSIS) (Luxembourg, 7-9 April 2008)

Proposal for a New Generic Statistical Business Process Model. Working paper No. 10, Joint UNECE/Eurostat/OECD meeting on Management of Statistical Information Systems (MSIS) (Luxembourg, 7-9 April 2008)

Statistical Excellence Through Capability Development and Planning—ABS Organisational People and Learning System ECE/CES/2006/22, CONFERENCE OF EUROPEAN STATISTICIANS

Fifty-fourth Plenary Session, Paris, 13-15 June 2006 Strategy-based Human Resources Management in Practice—Experience of Statistics Finland ECE/CES/2006/14, CONFERENCE OF EUROPEAN STATISTICIANS Fifty-fourth Plenary Session, Paris, 13-15 June 2006.

2

Business Process Re-engineering for HR Managers

—Mr. Rookesh Kumar Misra*
—G. Chandrayya**

The analysis and design of workflows and processes within an organization. A business process is a set of logically related tasks performed to achieve a defined business outcome. Re-engineering is the basis for many recent developments in management. The cross-functional team, for example, has become popular because of the desire to re-engineer separate functional tasks into complete cross-functional processes. Also, many recent management information systems developments aim to integrate a wide number of business functions. Enterprise resource planning, supply chain management, knowledge management systems, groupware and

* H.R. Manager Hyderabad (A.P.)
** Lecturer in Commerce, Government College, Rajhamundry, East Godavari District, A.P.

collaborative systems. Human Resource Management Systems and customer relationship management.

Business Process Reengineering is also known as Business Process Redesign, Business Transformation, or Business Process Change Management.

Overview

Business process reengineering (BPR) began as a private sector technique to help organizations fundamentally rethink how they do their work in order to dramatically improve customer service, cut operational costs, and become world-class competitors. A key stimulus for reengineering has been the continuing development and deployment of sophisticated

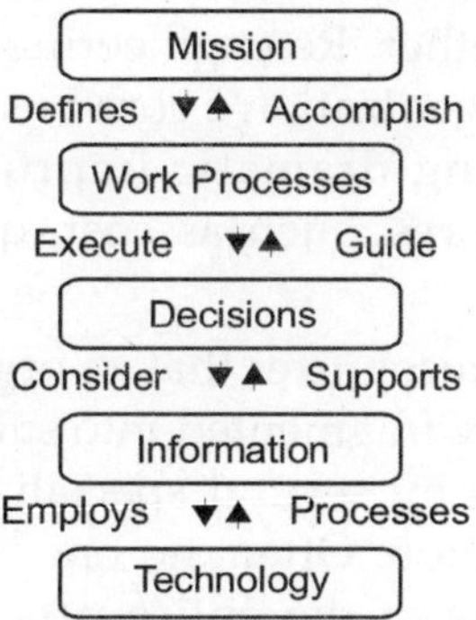

information systems and networks. Leading organizations are becoming bolder in using this technology to support innovative business processes, rather than refining current ways of doing work.

Re-engineering Guidance and Relationship of Mission and Work Processes to Information Technology: Business process re-engineering is one approach for redesigning the way work is done to better support the organization's mission and reduce costs. Re-engineering starts with a high-level assessment of the organization's mission, strategic goals, and customer needs. Basic questions are asked, such as "Does our mission need to be redefined? Are our strategic goals aligned with our mission? Who are our customers?" An organization may find that it is operating on questionable assumptions, particularly in terms of the wants and needs of its customers. Only after the organization rethinks what it should be doing, does it go on to decide how best to do it.

Within the framework of this basic assessment of mission and goals, re-engineering focuses on the organization's business processes—the steps and procedures that govern how resources are used to create products and services that meet the needs of particular. customers or markets. As a structured ordering of work steps across time and place, a business process can be decomposed into specific activities, measured, modelled, and improved. It can also be completely redesigned or eliminated altogether. Re-engineering identifies, analyzes, and redesigns an organization's core business processes with the aim of achieving dramatic improvements in critical performance measures, such as cost, quality, service, and speed.

Re-engineering recognizes that an organization's business processes are usually fragmented into subprocesses and tasks that are carried out by several specialized functional areas within the organization. Often, no one is responsible for the overall performance of the entire process. Re-engineering maintains that optimizing the performance of subprocesses can result in some benefits, but cannot yield dramatic improvements if the process itself is fundamentally inefficient and outmoded. For that reason, reengineering focuses on redesigning the process as a whole in order to achieve the greatest possible benefits to the organization and their customers. This drive for realizing dramatic improvements by fundamentally rethinking how the organization's work should be done distinguishes re-engineering from process improvement efforts that focus on functional or incremental improvement.

History

In 1990, Michael Hammer, a former professor of computer science at the Massachusetts Institute of Technology (MIT), published an article in the *Harvard Business Review*, in which he claimed that the major challenge for managers is to obliterate non-value adding work, rather than using technology for automating it. This statement implicitly accused managers of having focused on the wrong issues, namely that technology in general, and more specifically information technology, has been used primarily for automating existing processes rather than using it as an enabler for making non-value adding work obsolete.

Hammer's claim was simple—Most of the work being done does not add any value for customers, and this work should be removed, not accelerated through automation. Instead, companies should reconsider their processes in order to maximize customer value, while minimizing the consumption of resources required for delivering their product or service. A similar idea was advocated by Thomas H. Davenport and J. Short in 1990, at that time a member of the Earnest and Young research centre, in a paper published in the *Sloan Management Review* the same year as Hammer published his paper.

This idea, to unbiasedly review a company's business processes, was rapidly adopted by a huge number of firms, which were striving for renewed competitiveness, which they had lost due to the market entrance of foreign competitors, their inability to satisfy customer needs, and their insufficient cost structure. Even well established management thinkers, such as Peter Drucker and Tom Peters, were accepting and advocating BPR as a new tool for (re-)achieving success in a dynamic world. During the following years, a fast growing number of publications, books as well as journal articles, were dedicated to BPR, and many consulting firms embarked on this trend and developed BPR methods. However, the critics were fast to claim that BPR was a way to dehumanize the work place, increase managerial control, and to justify downsizing, i.e. major reductions of the work force, and a rebirth of Taylorism under a different label.

Despite this critique, reengineering was adopted at an accelerating pace and by 1993, as many as 65 per cent of the Fortune 500 companies claimed to either have initiated reengineering efforts, or to have plans to do so. This trend was fueled by the fast adoption of BPR by the consulting industry, but also by the study *Made in America,* conducted by MIT, that showed how companies in many US industries had lagged behind their foreign counterparts in terms of competitiveness, time-to-market and productivity.

Development after 1995

With the publication of critiques in 1995 and 1996 by some of the early BPR proponents, coupled with abuses and misuses of the concept by others, the reengineering fervor in the U.S. began to wane. Since then, considering business processes as a starting point for business analysis and redesign has become a widely accepted approach and is a standard part of the change methodology portfolio, but is typically performed in a less radical way as originally proposed.

More recently, the concept of Business Process Management (BPM) has gained major attention in the corporate world and can be considered as a successor to the BPR wave of the 1990s, as it is evenly driven by a striving for process efficiency supported by information technology. Equivalently to the critique brought forward against BPR, BPM is now accused of focussing on technology and disregarding the people aspects of change.

Business Process Re-engineering Topics

Definition

Different definitions can be found. This section contains the definition provided in notable publications in the field:

- "... the fundamental rethinking and radical redesign of business processes to achieve dramatic improvements in critical contemporary measures of performance, such as cost, quality, service, and speed."
- "encompasses the envisioning of new work strategies, the actual process design activity, and the implementation of the change in all its complex technological, human, and organizational dimensions."

Additionally, Davenport (ibid.) points out the major difference between BPR and other approaches to organization development (OD), especially the continuous improvement or TQM movement, when he states: "Today firms must seek not fractional, but multiplicative levels of improvement—10x rather than 10 per cent." Finally, Johansson provide a description of BPR relative to other process-oriented views, such as Total Quality Management (TQM) and Just-in-time (JIT), and state:

- "Business Process Re-engineering, although a close relative, seeks radical rather than merely continuous improvement. It escalates the efforts of JIT and TQM to make process orientation a strategic tool and a core competence of the organization. BPR concentrates on core business processes, and uses the specific techniques within the JIT and TQM 'toolboxes' as enablers, while broadening the process vision."

In order to achieve the major improvements BPR is seeking for, the change of structural organizational variables, and other ways of managing and performing work is often considered as being insufficient. For being able to reap the achievable benefits fully, the use of information technology (IT) is conceived as a major contributing factor. While IT traditionally has been used for supporting the existing business functions, i.e. it was used for increasing organizational efficiency, it now plays a role as enabler of new organizational forms, and patterns of collaboration within and between organizations."

BPR derives its existence from different disciplines, and four major areas can be identified as being subjected to change in BPR—organization, technology, strategy, and people - where a process view is used as common framework for considering these dimensions. The approach can be graphically depicted by a modification of 'Leavitt's diamond'.

Business strategy is the primary driver of BPR initiatives and the other dimensions are governed by strategy's encompassing role. The organization dimension reflects the structural elements of the company, such as hierarchical levels, the composition of organizational units, and the distribution of work between them. Technology is concerned with the use of computer systems and other forms of communication technology in the business. In BPR, information technology is generally considered as playing a role as enabler of new forms of organizing and collaborating, rather than supporting existing business functions. The people/human resources dimension deals with aspects such as education, training, motivation and reward systems. The concept of business processes—interrelated activities aiming at creating a value added output to a customer—is the basic underlying idea of BPR. These processes are characterized by a number of attributes: Process ownership, customer focus, value adding, and cross-functionality.

The Role of Information Technology

Information technology (IT) has historically played an important role in the reengineering concept. It is considered by some as a major enabler for new forms of working and collaborating within an organization and across organizational borders.

Early BPR literature identified several so called *disruptive technologies* that were supposed to challenge traditional wisdom about how work should be performed.

- Shared databases, making information available at many places
- Expert systems, allowing generalists to perform specialist tasks
- Telecommunication networks, allowing organizations to be centralized and decentralized at the same time
- Decision-support tools, allowing decision-making to be a part of everybody's job
- Wireless data communication and portable computers, allowing field personnel to work office independent
- Interactive videodisk, to get in immediate contact with potential buyers
- Automatic identification and tracking, allowing things to tell where they are, instead of requiring to be found
- High performance computing, allowing on-the-fly planning and revisioning.

In the mid 1990s, especially workflow management systems were considered as a significant contributor to improved process efficiency. Also ERP (Enterprise Resource Planning) vendors, such as SAP, JD Edwards, Oracle, PeopleSoft, positioned their solutions as vehicles for business process redesign and improvement.

Research and Methodology

Although the labels and steps differ slightly, the early methodologies that were rooted in IT-centric BPR solutions share many of the same basic principles and elements. The following outline is one such model, based on the PRLC (Process Reengineering Life Cycle) approach developed by Guha.

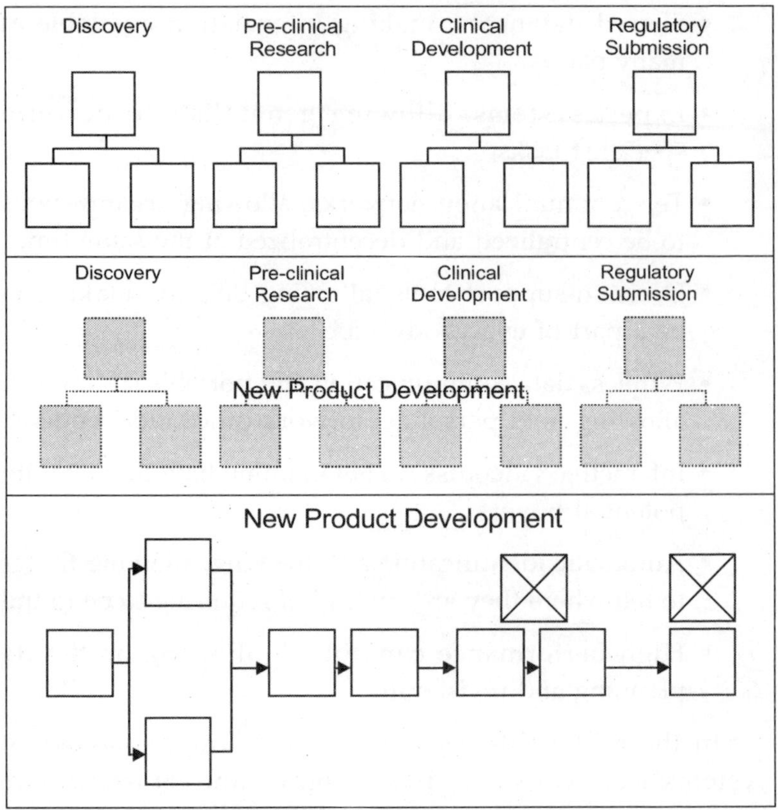

Simplified schematic outline of using a business process approach, examplified for pharmaceutical R&D:

1. Structural organization with functional units
2. Introduction of New Product Development as cross-functional process
3. Re-structuring and streamlining activities, removal of non-value adding tasks.

Benefiting from lessons learned from the early adopters, some BPR practitioners advocated a change in emphasis to a customer-centric, as opposed to an IT-centric, methodology. One such methodology, that also incorporated a Risk and

Impact Assessment to account for the impact that BPR can have on jobs and operations, was described by Lon Roberts (1994). Roberts also stressed the use of change management tools to proactively address resistance to change—a factor linked to the demise of many reengineering initiatives that looked good on the drawing board.

Some items to use on a process analysis checklist are: Reduce handoffs. Centralize data, Reduce delays, Free resources faster, Combine similar activities. Also within the management consulting industry, a significant number of methodological approaches have been developed.

Critique

Reengineering has earned a bad reputation because such projects have often resulted in massive layoffs. This reputation is not altogether unwarranted, since companies have often downsized under the banner of reengineering. Further, reenginecring has not always lived up to its expectations. The main reasons seem to be that:

- Reengineering assumes that the factor that limits an organization's performance is the ineffectiveness of its processes (which may or may not be true) and offers no means of validating that assumption.
- Reengineering assumes the need to start the process of performance improvement with a 'clean slate,' i.e. totally disregard the *status quo*.
- According to *Eliyahu M. Goldratt* (and his *Theory of Constraints*) reengineering does not provide an effective way to focus improvement efforts on the organization's constraint.

There was considerable hype surrounding the introduction of *Reengineering the Corporation* (partially due to *the fact* that the authors of the book reportedly bought numbers of copies to promote it to the top of bestseller lists).

Abrahamson (1996) showed that fashionable management terms tend to follow a lifecycle, which for Re-engineering peaked between 1993 and 1996 (Ponzi and Koenig 2002). They argue that Re-engineering was in fact nothing new (as e.g. when Henry Ford implemented the assembly line in 1908, he was in fact re-engineering, radically changing the way of thinking in an organization). Dubois (2002) highlights the value of signaling terms as Re-engineering, giving it a name, and stimulating it. At the same there can be a danger in usage of such fashionable concepts as mere ammunition to implement particular reform. Read Article by Faraz Rafique. The most frequent and harsh critique against BPR concerns the strict focus on efficiency and technology and the disregard of people in the organization that is subjected to a re-engineering initiative. Very often, the label BPR was used for major workforce reductions. Thomas Davenport, an early BPR proponent, stated that:

> "When I wrote about 'business process redesign' in 1990, explicitly said that using it for cost reduction alone was not a sensible goal. And consultants Michael Hammer and James Champy, the two names most closely associated with re-engineering. have insisted all along that layoffs shouldn't be the point. But the fact is. once out of the bottle, the re-engineering genie quickly turned ugly."

Michael Hammer similarly admitted that:

> "I wasn't smart enough about that, I was reflecting my engineering background and was insufficient appreciative of the human dimension. I've learned that's critical."

Other criticism brought forward against the BPR concept include:

- It never changed management thinking, actually the largest causes of failure in an organization.
- lack of management support for the initiative and thus poor acceptance in the organization.

- exaggerated expectations regarding the potential benefits from a BPR initiative and consequently failure to achieve the expected results.
- underestimation of the resistance to change within the organization.
- implementation of generic so-called best-practice processes that do nol fit specific company needs.
- overtrust in technology solutions.
- performing BPR as a one-off project with limited strategy alignment and long-term perspective.
- poor project management.

3

Re-engineering in Human Resource Management

—Dr. D. Tata Rao*

This article reviews the Business Process Re-engineering (BPR) vision of radical business process change, focussing upon the use of information technology to facilitate a shift away from linear/sequential work organization towards parallel processing and multidisciplinary teamworking. It highlights BPR's cursory treatment of the human dimension of its programme for radical organizational change and raises the question of how HRM specialists are to respond to its trivialisation of the complexities and dilemmas associated with the re-engineering of work processes.

Introduction

There is a new-look menu over at the Consultants' Cafe. Good old soupe du TQM and change management pate are off.

* Senior Faculty Department of Commerce Govt. Degree College, Yelamancheli, Visakhapatnama District Andhra University, A.P.

Perhaps you would care to try some business process re-engineering instead?'

During the 1980s, executives were invited to sample and digest a series of 'recipes' for enhancing corporate performance. Notably, they were urged by Peters and Waterman to emulate the successes of 'excellent' companies by strengthening their corporate cultures. More recently, Total Quality Management (TQM) has been widely promoted and adopted as a means of achieving continuous improvements.

However, a recent study indicates that around 85 per cent of the organizations using TQM are disappointed with the outcome .... experts are predicting that TQM will be replaced by corporate re-engineering as the technique most favoured by organizations anxious to maximise their people and material resources. In order to compete successfully against 'sleek startups and streamlined Japanese companies', Hammer, the leading advocate of Business Process Re-engineering (BPR), asserts that 'companies need fast change and dramatic improvements'. In BPR, the emphasis is placed upon the potential of Information and Communication Technologies (ICTs) to play a key, enabling role in transforming the design of work processes, a role that stretches far beyond the automation of existing methods of manufacturing products or delivering services. 'Nearly all our processes originated before the advent of modern computer and communications technology. They are replete with mechanisms designed to compensate for 'information poverty'. Although we are now information affluent, we still use those mechanisms, which are now deeply embedded in automated systems' ICTs are identified as a means of quite radically 'reengineering' organizations to achieve market responsiveness whilst substantially reducing labour costs. Making the transition from functions centred to process-oriented organizing practices necessarily depends upon the 'human resources' who enact, and are also (re)constituted by, BPR. Given BPR's focus upon business processes, it is remarkable how little attention is given by BPR to the human dimensions of organizing. The paper begins by reviewing the

BPR vision of radical business process change, focusing upon its use of information technology to facilitate a move away from linear/sequential work organization towards parallel processing and multidisciplinary teamworking. The neglect of the human dimension within BPR is then identified. Finally, the paper questions how HRM specialists, in particular, are to respond to its trivialisation of the human and organizational complexities and dilemmas associated with the BPR recipe for radical organizational change. It concludes by suggesting that the human aspects and implications of BPR have been woefully neglected, and that these should provide a strong focus for contemporary management research.

Business Panaceas Revisited?

Given the number and variety of earlier solutions to unsatisfactory corporate performance that failed to fulfil their promise, it is not surprising to discover a degree of scepticism about Business Process Reengineering (BPR), especially as its programmatic and abstract character makes it harder to pin down than recipes for strengthening corporate culture or building quality into every aspect of business activity. Does BPR have a distinctive flavour or is it the same old imperialistic consultancy guff dressed up in new jargon? Needless to say, business consultants have a vested interest in emphasising the novelty and potency of whatever variety of 'snake oil' they dispense to managers. But investment in previous recipes also means that they are inclined to interpret the new in terms of the old, and to repackage old wine in new bottles. In turn, this may lead to an overhasty dismissal of BPR as simply the latest in a line of fads that is distinguished from previous panaceas only by its achievement of a new nadir in the inelegance of its terminology. In our view, such treatment is unhelpful if it blinds us to the possibility that BPR represents and promotes something distinctive and innovative in its approach to the restructuring of business practices. In common with previous recipes for improving business performance—

from Taylorism to TQM-BPR draws together, synthesises and provides an articulation for ideas and practices that have been floating around in the business world without a catchy label or a champion. Though it may represent a new nadir in the inelegance of its terminology, BPR is sufficiently striking, flexible and ambiguous to encompass many programmes and techniques, such as teamworking, and networking and even EPOS (electronic point of sale), that have contributed to the reorganization of work during the 1980s. What Hammer has done is not so much to concoct a novel recipe but to put a name to an emergent trend in business organization that has been prompted, above all, by an intensification of competition that intensifies the pressures upon executives to seek (radical) ways of gaining competitive advantage. His contribution, like that of earlier guru figures, resides in a flair for packaging and promoting an appealing product in a market where status-conscious consumers are, like the proverbial Emperor, anxious to espouse and sport the latest in management fashions.

Hammer's formulation of BPR promises radical (not just incremental) improvements in such areas as product development, product quality and speed of delivery. By undertaking a fundamental review and transformation of key business processes, Hammer's focus is upon the leaps in performance that can be attained through the innovative use of ICTs. Instead of using ICTs to 'automate' existing, functionally organized methods of production, Hammer urges that they be mobilised to redesign processes in ways that 'obliterate' established practices. 'It is time to stop paving the cow paths. Instead of embedding outdated processes in silicon and software, we should obliterate them and start over. We should 're-engineer' our businesses : use the power of modern information technology to radically redesign our business processes in order to achieve dramatic improvements in their performance'.

The embeddedness of out-moded mechanisms both within organization structures and their IT systems is diagnosed as a principal source of competitive decline. Their symptoms are legion : lengthy product development cycles, poor customer responsiveness and service, capital locked up in operations that add little or no value. Even in companies that have embraced the principles of TQM and JIT, it is claimed that their bureaucratic structures have been left largely intact, or have even been reinforced by such programmes, making possible room for dramatic improvements in performance 'Despite (the application of TQM and JIT principles), most Western companies remain highly bureaucratic, with departments acting individually and 'throwing over the wall' to the next department designs, information, product, and most of all problems ..... barriers to overall business effectiveness are raised and turf is jealously guarded .... This kind of organizational linking needs to be broken apart and rebuilt as a process-oriented business .... where everyone regards working in cross-functional teams as the norm .... and where everyone knows that the key goal is to produce a service or product that the marketplace perceives to be best' BPR demands that old assumptions, values and rules, are challenged and superseded. For example, BPR encourages a fundamental questioning of conventional wisdoms—such as the assumption that merchandising decisions are best made at headquarters; or that customers don't (and perhaps won't) make even straightforward repairs to their own electrical equipment. It is by exposing and overthrowing assumptions that lock companies into existing paradigms of production and distribution that BPR promises to accomplish the quantum leaps in processes of service delivery, product development cycles, etc.

Instead of striving to make incremental improvements to existing processes, BPR urges the radical re-examination of current practice in order to 'determine which of its steps really add value and search for new ways to achieve the result'. To take the analogy of new product development, the BPR approach favours the development of a completely new product rather than one that improves marginally upon existing products. Recent examples, taken from the financial services industry, are the development of Direct Line insurance sales and the establishment of Firstdirect as an alternative to conventional banking. Both innovations rely heavily upon ICTs to gain a niche within a saturated and highly competitive market place. With the UK, N & P Building Society is perhaps the most celebrated case of a financial services organization that has triumphantly embraced the BPR credo. The application of BPR may be confined to one area of activity—for example, the delivery of a particular product or to the development of an alternative product. But it is also, and more fundamentally, concerned with revolutionising all kinds of established organizational practices in an effort to achieve dramatic, 'quantum leaps' in business performance. We cannot achieve breakthroughs in performance by cutting fat or automating existing processes. Rather, we must challenge old assumptions and shed the old rules that made the business underperform in the first place' Radical transformation is possible, the advocates of BPR argue, because most businesses continue to rely upon structures and procedures that pre-date the processing capabilities of low cost ICTs. It is by thinking carefully about how new, alternative modes of operation can harness the power of ICTs that breakthroughs can be achieved.

De-differentiating the Collective Worker

When it comes to identifying the new organizing practices that are to replace old, outmoded mechanisms, the advocates of BPR are more vague and its methodology of change is quite opaque. Not undeservedly, BPR has been likened to the curry house special : no one knows exactly what it is. However, certain contours are comparatively well defined. BPR's special weapon is the power of ICTs and its principal targets are functionally-based structures and sequentially organized processes. Both are criticised for their tendency to differentiate rather than integrate elements of product design, manufacture and delivery. As Hammer and Champy make this case, The most basic and common feature of re-engineered processes is the absence of an assembly line; that is, many formerly distinct jobs or tasks are integrated and compressed into one'.

The call for improved integration is hardly unique. Improved flexibility and responsiveness and the reduction of managerial overhead, both to be accomplished through the de-differentiation of what Marx terms the collective worker, is a recurrent theme of the new management thinking. Kanter (1992) has described 'post-entrepreneurial' companies that are successful in achieving improved integration (trans : de-differentiation) in the following terms. They make sure each area contributes something to the others. The leaner, more focussed, more cooperative and integrated organizations that result help each unit add value to the others. The 'whole' contributes something above and beyond the value of the parts .... The post-entrepreneurial corporation represents a triumph of process over structure. That is, relationships and communication and the flexibility to temporarily combine resources are more important that the 'formal' channels and reporting relationships represented on an organizational chart'. The understanding that there is an alternative to the classical, bureaucratic form of corporate design can be traced back at least as far as Burns and Stalker's The Management of Innovation (1961). Burns and Stalker argued that a more dynamic, 'organic' system of management was appropriate for companies operating in environments that frequently gave rise to fresh, unanticipated and unpredictable problems. The difference today is that leading management gurus, including the champions of BPR, are insisting that virtually all companies can only hope to survive if they rapidly develop systems that match and surpass the re-engineered, post-entrepreneurial organizing methods that have been pioneered or adopted by the most successful companies, including many market leaders.

At the heart of new management thinking, including BPR, is a concern to remedy a familiar subject of industrial sociology: the problem of goal displacement and organizational politics. Corporate goals become displaced when the occupants of functional specialisms become preoccupied with their own objectives and/or devote themselves to the specific range of responsibilities allotted to their specialism, to the neglect of their contribution to adding value to the corporation as a whole. In common with other recipes for improving corporate performance, a key objective of BPR is to challenge and disrupt such 'dysfunctional' patterns of behaviour. But BPR is distinctive in urging the use of ICTs to de-differentiate tasks that have been dispersed into discrete functions or steps in a process. ICTs are understood to provide the technological means of running in parallel tasks or processes that were previously organized in series. At one level, then, advocates of BPR can be said to be labelling old wine into new bottles. But, at another level they are making a radical and indeed extraordinary claim. Namely, that the chronic managerial problem of achieving a balance between differentiation (to cope with task complexity) and integration (to coordinate a fragmented division of labour) can be solved by using ICTs to re-engineer business processes so that a single individual, or a virtual individual comprising a group of employees linked in real time by ICTs, can perform tasks that previously were divided between a number of imperfectly coordinated staff. Whereas the old principles of work organization tended to assume the necessity for functional departments that were accountable, through hierarchical organization, to themselves. The new principle says to forge links between parallel functions and to coordinate them while their activities are in process rather than after they are completed. Communications networks, shared data bases, and teleconferencing can bring the independent groups together so that coordination is on-going' But it seeks to deploy ICTs to reduce both vertical and horizontal divisions wherever these do not 'add value'. As this occurs, the accountability of specialists shifts from their function within the hierarchy to the task or project in process. Instead of complying with the standards of performance demanded by their specialist function, employees are required to direct and discipline their efforts in accordance with the demands of the task. In principle, the multifunctional group determines, guides and evaluates the contribution of each member. These groups are also required to feedback and inform the development of the broad priorities in a more direct and open manner than has hitherto been achieved. However, hierarchical relations continue to set broad priorities and monitor their performance with the assistance of information technology.

A Preliminary Assessment

The experience or threat of losing market share makes BPR potentially appealing to senior executives who are attracted by the claims of a technique that promises to make a quantum leap beyond the performance gains delivered by the Japanese lead in JIT and TQM. On the other hand, it could be objected that the BPR focus is upon improving the operations of companies, to the possible neglect of the competitive advantages that can be gained from other sources, such as strategic planning and marketing. This objection is partially disarmed by Hammer's insistence that management functions, including marketing, be integrated into processes of product development, etc. BPR could be deployed to reengineer the processes through which corporate strategies are formulated and implemented, but it does not extend to identifying or creating markets or niches where big profits can be made. BPR is presented primarily an operations-led approach to strategic self-improvement. It builds upon, as it aspires to leap beyond, 'the tactical process-oriented philosophies of JIT and TQM .... to bring the process philosophy into the broader realm of corporate strategy. BPR has most relevance for securing and defending niches by continuously (re)engineering processes so that profit levels can be sustained even if there is a decision to increase costs (e.g. by enhancing the product or raising the marketing spend) or reduce prices in order to maintain market share. It is not an alternative to strategic management. BPR presents a novel challenge to organisational structures, processes and cultures. But its promise of greater productivity and shorter time to market is predicated on making major shifts in managerial practice and culture, the attainment of which is brushed aside in the BPR literature. Whilst advocating multidisciplinary integration of business processes, it is largely driven by the logic and language of computer science and production engineering. Perhaps for this reason, if no other, David Nadler, president of Delta Consulting Group is reported to have said that We have watched a number of re-engineering projects fail. They have involved huge promises of savings, but have either stopped because they don't seem to be leading anywhere, or they have been completed but with none of the promised gains to show for it. Moreover, such projects generate payments to consultants of upward of $5 to $20 million. It's a nasty little secret'. By promising to provide the means of leaping ahead of the global competition, the BPR vision of the future of work presents a beguiling answer to the problems of declining competitiveness. However, it also promotes the continuing contraction of employment as organizations (continuously) reengineer their processes. Those who remain are obliged to work at an everquickening intensity and pace. For this elite, there is the prospect of eventual 'burnout' and disposal. For the mass whose jobs have been re-engineered out of these companies, there is the increasingly restricted prospect of occupying the lowly paid, temporary jobs that service tomorrow's 'networkers' 'information brokers' and 'symbolic analysts'. This is the achilles heel of BPR. Implicitly, employees are assumed to be BPR to be infinitely malleable. And any antagonism to BPR is interpreted as inertia rather than as warrantable resistance to change that can be dissolved by the persuasive powers of senior management. HRM specialists, in particular, may question whether the ambitions of BPR are consistent with the distinctive qualities of 'human resources'. More specifically, it might be asked to what extent the increased pressures that are fuelled by BPR are compatible with ideas of creativity, empowerment and fulfilment that differentiate human beings from other factors of production. From this perspective, it is not BPR's inflated sense of novelty so much as its shallow, technicist appreciation of the human dimension of organisational change that renders it vulnerable to failure and must be addressed, not least by HRM specialists. Two contrasting responses can be identified, depending upon how the distinctive identity concerns of HRM are formulated. If the responsibilities of the HRM specialist are construed primarily in terms of facilitating change programmes designed and initiated by others, then a relevant response to the alleged deficiencies of BPR would be to propose refinements that incorporate HRM techniques that are tailored to the adoption of BPR and/or overcoming resistance to its implementation. On the other hand, if HRM specialists aspire to some degree of professional (including ethical) autonomy, however partial and precarious, they may question whether the assumptions and ambitions of BPR are consistent with enhancing the qualities of creativity, empowerment and fulfilment that differentiate human beings from other factors of production. A major problem with the intent of BPR, as its critics have observed, is that its celebration of the idea of unbridled competitiveness as an unassailable good 'locks us into a frenzied cycle of growth with desperate environmental consequences...competition does not just exist as some transcendental condition but is the outcome of practices, of which BPR is the latest variant. It is as if a person were running on a treadmill being constantly encouraged to run faster to keep up with the wheel'. How are HRM specialists to respond to the challenges of BPR, including its contribution to unemployment and its intensification of work processes? Is their professional understanding of the distinctiveness qualities of the human resource to be applied to smooth the passage for a (technocratic) mode of change management that is divisive in terms of its effects upon employment, and which either disregards or trivializes the distinctiveness of the human resource? If so, the HRM specialist surely deserve the epithetic pimp of management—in the sense of procuring human resources for economic exploitation without regard for the moral basis of social and economic relations, or the demoralising effects of treating human beings as manipulable, expendable resources. For, instead of questioning and challenging the pressures to reduce human beings to commodities, HRM specialists contrive to use their specialist knowledge of the 'human resource' to represent its commodification as entirely normal and legitimate. Or are HRM specialists to develop and apply their expertise in ways that expose and explore the basic conflicts between a system driven by impersonal imperatives for profit and growth? In which case, the radical claims of BPR are questioned on the grounds that it is seen to 'hijack the notion of radicalism in the service of aims that are politically conservative'—for example, by debasing the (radical) currency of empowerment as it is equated with the idea that those remaining in employment can be empowered (as if it empowerment were a gift to be bestowed by others) to ensure the smoother operation of a system that systematically exploits and oppresses in the name of individual freedom and opportunity.

Hammering the Human Resource

The marginalization and trivialization of the human dimension from expositions of BPR is remarkable, even by the standards of leading proponents of TQM. Making the transition from function-centred to process-oriented organizing practices necessarily depends upon the 'human resources' who enact, and are enacted by, BRP. Given the focus upon business processes, it is incredible how little attention is given by BPR to the human dimensions of organizing. This shortcoming is symptomatic of the way BPR's claims and prescriptions for change are even more abstracted from the practical realities of organizing and managing people than earlier recipes for improving business performance, such as Excellence and TQM. Little consideration is given to the issue of how BPR's (universal) remedies are to be reconciled with the (particular) conditions in which its prescriptions are to be applied.

When examples are given, these are presented as unequivocal success stories. For example, Hammer describes how Ford (North America) reduced its accounts payable staff from 500+ to 125 by redesigning the payment process and using ICTs in a way that dispensed with invoices altogether. Perhaps those who lost their jobs (or were redeployed) were entirely supportive and cooperative in this change. In this respect at least, the parallels between BPR and Taylorism are quite striking. Like Taylor, who rose to become Chief Engineer at the Midvale Steel Company, Hammer, the computer scientist, is quick to transfer the language of computing, and recent developments in parallel processing, to the complex and frequently perverse world of human relations. In any event, Hammer unreservedly represents the re-engineered process as a means of 'empowering' employees. When commenting upon the re-engineering of insurance applications at US Insurer Mutual Benefit Life (MBL), for instance, he observes that 'empowering individuals to process entire applications ..... has eliminated 100 field office positions, and case managers can handle more than twice the volume of new applications the company previously could process'. Here empowerment is equated with the integration of tasks made possible by the development of expert systems and relational data bases rather than with the expansion of discretion or even an increase in task variety. No consideration is given to the loss of employment opportunities associated with such change. Nor does Hammer consider the probability that the VDU operators ('case managers') are stuck in a dead-end job that in all likelihood has become more intensive, routine and isolating as a consequence of the re-engineering. Indeed, virtually the only comment made by Hammer on the human dimension of BPR is that its demands upon employees are entirely congruent with an educated (trans.: self-disciplined) workforce that no longer requires close supervision. What methods are used to 'produce' this workforce remain a mystery. The population in general is simply deemed to be 'capable of assuming responsibility, cherish their autonomy and expect to have a say in how the business is run'. Consider the situation of the 'case managers' at MBL. Assuming that the tasks which they performed were driven by menus, it is difficult to reconcile the highly routinized design of their work with 'assuming responsibility'. If employees do indeed 'cherish their autonomy', it would be interesting to discover how MBL retained these 'case managers'. Finally, it would be instructive to know what 'say' they had in running the business. For example, what involvement can they expect to have in any future 'reengineering process' that might further intensify their work or 'eliminate their positions'? Champions of BPR, like Taylor again, are willing to acknowledge that the radical changes envisaged by BPR may encounter some resistance. But they also assume that this resistance can be dissolved by effective leadership and commitment from top management. Hammer, for example, acknowledges that the disruption and confusion generated by re-engineering can make it unpopular, though he is equally confident that any opposition can be effectively surmounted by top-level managers. The commitment of managers as champions of BPR is deemed to be sufficient 'to enlist those who would prefer the status quo'. So, despite an admission that 'the strain of implementing a re-engineering plan can hardly be overestimated', Hammer is sure that employees can be convinced of its virtues; or, to put this more directly, where major job losses are involved, he is confident that strong leadership can persuade sufficient turkeys to vote for Christmas. In a recent Harvard Business Review article that reviews the experience of BPR in 100 companies, with detailed consideration to its application in 20 companies, a rather less sanguine conclusion is reached. Once again, it is assumed that 'strong leadership from management' is necessary if BPR projects are not to be sabotaged by 'the psychological and political disruptions that accompany such radical change'. However, there is a greater appreciation both of the depth of this resistance and the scale of resources and length of time required to accomplish radical organisational transformation: 'all the old support systems will become obsolete—from IT systems to employee skills ... The new infrastructure should include programmes like comprehensive training and skill development plans that require years, not merely months, for success; performance—measurement systems that track how well the organisation is meeting its targets and how employees should be rewarded-based on those objectives; communication programmes that help employees understand how and why their behaviour must change ..... Here there is some awareness of how employees, not just processes, must be re-engineered or debugged if they are to run effectively in the systems. However, there remains the assumption that employees, including managers, are infinitely malleable; that the parallel development of HRM systems and strong leadership will dissolve resistance; and that the new systems will not themselves generate new problems and resistances. What such assessments and prescriptions omit or, at best, marginalise is an appreciation of BPR's major implications for job losses and further intensification/degradation of the quality of working life for employees at all levels. Which does not mean that some features of the changes envisaged by process reengineering will not be welcomed. For example, despite the increased routinization and depersonalization of their work, 'case managers' at MBL (see above) may approve of the removal of supervisors or prefer the reduced fragmentation of tasks. But even those who, on balance, endorse such changes are also likely to have reservations about its implications for their future job security. They may also recognise, and resent, the extent to which the pace and accuracy of their work can now be continuously monitored, albeit indirectly, by information systems. Hammer himself acknowledges that the reengineering of business processes has numerous implications for how businesses are managed. For example, he notes that the introduction of the new process of handling applications at MBL necessitated some major changes: 'MBL had to develop a culture in which people doing work are perceived as more important than those supervising work. Career paths, recruitment and training programmes, promotion policies—these and many other management systems are being revised to support the new process design'. However, despite the realization that new business processes can have knock-on effects upon the management of human resources, the implementation of changes necessary to support the new processes is presented as wholly unproblematical. Indeed, there seems to be an assumption of an elective affinity between so-called empowered employees, sophisticated systems of actual or potential surveillance and strong, and some might say demagogical, leadership in post-entrepreneurial organizations, as exemplified by T.J. Rogers, CEO at US chip producer Cypress Semiconductor since 1983. Rogers has advocated the empowering techniques of networking and teamworking. But he also runs an IT-based monitoring system that allows him to 'peer down into the bowels of the organization' and target the performance of individual employees. Even sympathetic commentators have described his managerial style as idiosyncratic and military. Because employees are not infinitely malleable, passive commodities who are indifferent to how they are managed, accomplishing the full and effective implementation of BPR is likely to prove more difficult than is contemplated by its advocates' faith in the persuasive powers of senior management. Where employee cooperation with the implementation of BPR is achieved under duress, it is likely that its impact will be sustained only by the same old coercive methods condemned by the new prophets of business management. Given the challenge BPR can present to established orders, processes and identities, an attentiveness to the insights of HRM would seem to be pertinent. However, this would require the prophets of BPR to acknowledge the shortcomings of their own specialist training, work cooperatively and openly with other functions, and thereby re-assess the value as well as the plausibility of their prescriptions.

Conclusion

Neglect of the human dimension in BPR may reflect a growing sense of confidence and/or desperation amongst corporate executives and their consultants. Confidence inasmuch that the 1980s have seen a successful employer offensive, supported by New Right industrial policy, that has weakened the power of employees to promote as well as resist change. But desperation too because this weakening of employee power has not been sufficient to reverse the loss of competitiveness and market share to Japanese businesses and Pacific Rim companies. Commercially speaking, it may be true that many companies struggling to survive in national and world markets are 'burdened' with 'layers of unproductive overhead and armies of unproductive workers' in comparison to their competitors. It may also be true that other 'softer' and more incremental recipes for (re)gaining competitive advantage have not done enough to lighten this burden. But it remains questionable whether those who comprise the 'overhead'—corporate managers no less than other employees—will willingly recognise themselves, or even be persuaded to understand themselves, either as a 'burden' or as 'unproductive'. Unlike previous recipes for organizational change championed by the gurus of Corporate Culture and TQM, BPR goes beyond declaring war upon supervisory and middle levels of management to attack head-on the very functional structures that have traditionally provided an identity and a career path for the managers that have formed an integral part of the collective worker. For this reason, amongst others, BPR is likely to encounter difficulties of implementation even where employees overtly espouse its objectives. It is not just that the 'process' thinking advocated by BPR is often foreign to those who are being required to apply it. It also poses an immediate or deferred threat to job security and conditions of work. Yet, the architects and advocates of BPR continue to assume either that employees will unequivocally welcome the changes brought by BPR or will be persuaded by top management to support them. As a consequence, there is no discussion of why, or how, managers and other employees may directly or covertly oppose its logic or resist its demands for change. This then raises the question of how HRM specialists are to address BPR's neglect and trivialization of the human dimensions of organizing and managing change. Are HRM specialists content simply to provide the relevant HR techniques that are claimed to smooth the implementation of programmes that have been designed by others? Or does their distinctive concern for the human dimension of work enable and spur them to question the rationality of remedies that contribute to the disease for which they profess to dispense a cure? The introduction of BPR in organizations will be as much a test of the meaning of professional ethics for the HRM specialists as it will be a trial for those who are subjected to, or displaced by, its zeal to obliterate jobs as well as established practices.

Acknowledgement I would like to thank Fergus Murray for his assistance and comments in preparing an earlier version of this paper as well as the helpful and constructive comments received from Chris Grey and anonymous referees.

4

Re-engineering in Higher Education *Reinventing Teaching and Learning*

—Dr. H. Srinivas Rao*

Introduction

Re-engineering has been discovered in the last 15 years by evaluating patterns of actions of companies and universities that had dramatic success in processes compared to those that failed to achieve a new way of operations. If we look back to all innovations, visions, models and theories which affected our life, work and operation, we can call all those events as the re-engineering of their time and places. Adam Smith's revolutionary model of business Wealth of Nation (1776) was re-engineering two hundred years ago: Henry Ford's vision in the automobile industry was re-engineering in 1903; and John Stevens, father of railroad development, was re-engineering in 1825. Re-engineering is the best use of available technology to redesign current processes of business,

* Sr. Lecturer in Commerce, Badruka College of Commerce, Kachiguda, Hyderabad-500 027

education and government in order to achieve the mission of the organization.

The concept of re-engineering is how to convert from hierarchical to flat structure, how to prepare teams to achieve goals, how to change task-oriented employees to multidimensional workers, how to change managers from supervisor to coach, and how to change overall processes in order to be competitive in global economics.

Importance of the Paper

Successful re-engineering in higher education must begin with teaching and learning rather than administrative processes. Addressing educational processes first will naturally force as a reconsideration of such features like the student credit hour, faculty load, space utilization the academic calendar course scheduling institutional resources like technology along with the design of student faculty interaction.

Objectives of the Paper

The study has been carried out to fulfill the following objectives:

1. To review the reengineering in Academic operations.
2. To study the optimum utilization of infrastructural facilities.
3. To identify computers as reengineering recourses.
4. To highlight training for students by the educational institutions.

Methodology

For the purpose of this paper, secondary data have been used. The required data have been collected from various websites and published books. Under primary source the opinions collected from various heads of institutions in reach.

Re-engineering in Academic Operations

In the new paradigm, computer technology has a major role and contribution to the designing and implementation of the teacher-student-centered or student-centered model. Unfortunately, lack of attention to the human power (faculty) in the utilization of technology is the most important reason for failing most of the planning. Compared with all other resources, faculty is the only one that can direct and coordinate utilization of technology, in the classroom.

The theme is academic reengineering is divided into two separate sections. The first section, teaching and learning is divided into the technology in the classroom, faculty competency, and student competency. The second section is curriculum development.

Teaching and Learning

Today's teaching and learning is based on the educational computing technology. This educational computing refers not only to the hardware, instructional systems and management systems, but also includes the software that embrace the curriculum and the intelligence and ideologies that guide the use of computers in educational environments.

Technology

Technology by itself cannot satisfy university's objectives and generate the desired outcome from teaching and learning. Higher educational institutions should have adequate infrastructure for access and delivery in order to design and direct a technology oriented curriculum.

The minimum infrastructure are:

- Network access from dorms, classes, and off campus.
- Network connection to every faculty's offices.
- Network ports for students to connect their portable computers.
- Network access from computer labs.

- Computer labs equipped with needed computer hardware, software, and support team.
- Training center with multi-talented support staffs with 9:00 to 5:00 availability for all the faculty and students.
- Network with capability of real-time video conferencing, multimedia, and rapid movement of large amounts of data.
- Capable workstation in every faculty's office and in the labs.
- Faculty development labs with hardware and software (scanner, audio and video editing) allowing rapid and high quality development.
- Support team that can participate and contribute to the more complicated developments.

Faculty Competency

Faculty Development is the critical key for opening the new world of learning to the students. If an institution's faculty is competent and comfortable with technology, that institution will have remarkable success in using technology in curriculum. Faculty can envision what technologies to use in the curriculum and why institutions should use those technologies. The major questions is how to prepare faculty for this change. The first and last rule is to provide learning options and let faculty make decisions about learning. The following are some of my suggestions:

- Create a plan for continuous systematic investigation of faculty and student learning needs.
- Create a learning centre with a multi-dimensional staff to help faculty to learn.
- Create ongoing workshops for department-wise, based on the department's need assessments and evaluations.
- Create opportunities for one on one training, based on the faculty's request.

- Provide free time for interested and committed faculty to develop computer-based curriculum.
- Strengthen your academic consultation and support groups.
- Strengthen your academic application development group.
- Design a faculty development grant programme for using technology in the curriculum.
- Create reward system for innovative use of computers in the curriculum.

Student Competency

In today's teaching and learning, most students use internet application for access to educational resources and e-mail is a common part of communication with teacher or other students. A few years ago we were worried that we are using computer only as super typewriter, but today we are worrying about using computer only for access and communication. Utilization of computer beyond, access tool by students has relation with competency and vision of faculty. Taking advantage of technology in the curriculum in the form of simulation, case study, intelligent system, and problem solver which are very important for the development of critical thinking and decision making skills.

Curriculum Design

In the curriculum design section, process oriented activities should be converted to outcome oriented activities with special attention to empowerment of students in learning activities. Technology should be part of the curriculum for accessing resources (library, internet applications), communication (e-mail, bulletin board), and computer based education applications (simulation, case study, and intelligent system).

Educational Institutions Training for Students

With the job market getting narrower, employers are being extremely choosing in the fresher market. Staying on top of the ever-changing industry standards can be tough, while a college degree gives the right qualification to a student. It must offer him to get the right job. Training modules have been designed to ensure that every student gets intellectually and professionally styled to suit the requirements of the job markets.

The mode of dealing with students include the following:

1. Assess the student's capabilities and personality.
2. Customize the training modules to suit the student.
3. Expose students to the requirements of Indian and global employers.
4. Impart short term intensive training programmes that career and employability skills.
5. Make them ready to win his dream job.
6. e-Leaming/e-communities and periodic mentoring during post training period.

Infrastructure and Learning Resources in Higher Educational Institutions

The system of higher education in India has expanded rapidly in the last 50 years. In spite of the built-in regulatory mechanisms that aim to ensure satisfactory levels of quality in the functioning of higher educational institutions, there has been criticisms that the country has permitted the mushrooming of institutions of higher education with unlimited programmes and substandard facilities and consequent dilution of standard. To address the issue of deterioration in quality, the National Policy on Education (1986) and the plan of action that spelt out the strategic plans for the policies, advocated the establishment of an independent national accreditation body. Consequently, the NAAC was established in 1994 with its headquarters at Bangalore.

Infrastructure plays a vital role in the quality of education. Our IITs are comparable, in standards to any of the leading institutions of the world. One of the reasons is the investment in them. They offer excellent facilities for teaching, learning and research. So, any attempt of the government to abdicate its responsibility to provide education to people will jeopardize education in a knowledgeable society. Apart from the government, earnest steps should be taken to rope in the local community to mobilize funds for the institutions.

In the present day, educational institution of higher learning is a complex task, especially when the social, economic and technological developments are rapidly changing the educational environment. Also, the increasing size and number of educational institutions across the country pose stiff competition in high education. In this context, it becomes an urgent need to think of introducing new, innovative and job-oriented courses in the years to come, considering the socio-economic and educational background of the people for whom the college has been established.

Maintain its Infrastructure

- The college has to watch and ward staff to guard and maintain the campus round the clock.
- The sweepers and scavengers should keep the campus clean and tidy.
- Uninterrupted and purified water supply should be ensured everyday.
- All the major repairs should done by the service agencies.
- The mechanic and laboratory assistant operate, maintain, repair and monitor the functioning of the generators.

- The gardener and the manual labourers keep the garden grove trim and tidy.
- The playgrounds are maintained and kept ready for sports and games.
- The college keeps the inventories of all the movable properties in the college. Every facility is recorded in the inventory. New additions and deletions are updated. Every item is given a unique number.
- A committee of selected staff does the stock verification every year internally and submits the report to the authorities.
- Damaged furniture is either repaired or replaced every year.
- A carpenter is appointed to carry out the repair and maintenance of the furniture as and when required.
- Buildings are whitewashed and blackboards are black-coated annually.
- The electrician and plumber look after their respective works whenever the need arises.
- Separate staff are appointed to operate Xerox copier, telephones, and televisions.
- A teaching staff-in-charge monitors and maintains the audio-visual aids with the help of the assistant.

Optimum Utilization of Its Infrastructural Facilities

(1) The classrooms are utilized for conducting:

- regular as well as self financing courses
- group discussions, seminars, quiz programmes, elocution and essay competitions
- class tests, centralized monthly tests, model examinations and university examinations

- various functions and association meetings of respective departments
- rehearsal of cultural events

(2) Science laboratories are used for:

- conducting regular practical classes
- demonstrating the experiments to inculcate the scientific inquiry
- arranging the science-scholars meet
- demonstrating motivational experiments to the nearby school children
- conducting experiments related to the research of the individual teachers

(3) The seminar hall is utilized for:

- departmental level seminars
- quiz programmes
- staff seminars
- management board meetings
- teaching and non-teaching staff meetings

(4) Playgrounds are used for the following purposes:

- regular sports and games
- the annual sports meet
- NCC parades
- inter-collegiate and zonal level tournaments
- NCC and NSS camps

(5) College and auditorium is used for conducting the following programmes:

- all the important functions like College Day, Fine Arts Day and association meetings
- orientation programmes for the fresher's
- general body meetings of alumni

Library and Information Services

Library is an essential component, where the collection, services and their out-reaching capacity is monitored. Libraries largely support learning, teaching and research processes in institutions.

Number of Days and Hours the Library is Kept Open

This is to help in knowing whether the library is kept open on Saturday, Sunday and other holidays so as to facilitate students and faculty. This parameter refers to opening and closing hours of the library, whether the library opens before the opening time of the institution and closes after the closing time so that readers have an opportunity to use the library without disturbance to their academic schedules.

Library Advisory Committee

The formation of the library committee with an equal representation by faculty and students, the role of the committee and its functions in developing the library services are to be well defined.

Manpower Development

Qualifications and the experience of the librarian and the library staff should be on par with that of the academic staff and should fulfill the norms prescribed by UGC/AICTE etc.

The library provides the following facilities/services to the students:

- publication and research support services
- information display and notification
- book bank
- internet
- audio-visual resources
- computers
- membership of library networks

Conclusion

The functioning of individual colleges could be maintained while insisting on the assessment of quality of all educational institutions in the country on the basis of a uniform criterion. This is not to argue that certain broad parameters of quality equally applicable to all institutions throughout the country cannot be arrived at by all. Indeed there is every reason to arrive at a national criterion and to insist on its realization in every institution in the country. But such broad indicators of quality relating to curriculum, teaching-learning and evaluation, infrastructure and learning resources, student support and progression, organization and management and healthy practices are only minimum requirements for the realization of excellence and do not automatically guarantee excellence etc. are the positive results of reengineering in higher educational institutions. The NAAC now rates individual institutions against standardized norms. The rating is given on the basis of internationally acceptable parameters.

REFERENCES

AIFUCTO—Teachers Movement, A Monthly Journal of AIFUCTO, Volume 8, Issue 1, January 2006.

Guidelines on Quality Indications in Library and Information Services published by NAAC (National Assessment and Accreditation Council) Bangalore 2005.

A Decade of Dedication to Quality Assurance Published by NAAC, Bangalore 2004.

Computer Fundamentals by P. Mohan, published by Himalaya Publishing House, Delhi 2006.

WWW. reengineering in high education by Bizhan Nasseh.

5

Re-engineering of Human Resource Management Research in Recent Trends

—G. Chandrayya*
—Dr. R.N. Misra**

The Human Resources function may set strategies and develop policies, standards, systems and processes to implement these strategies in a whole range of areas for which the following would be typical of a wide range of organizations:

1. Recruitment and Selection (Resourcing);
2. Organizational Design and Development;
3. Business Transformation and Change Management;
4. Performance, Conduct and Behaviour Management;
5. Industrial and Employee Relations;
6. Human Resources (or workforce) Analysis and the Management of Workforce Personal Data;

* Senior Lecturer, Department of Commerce Government College (Autonomous), Rajahmundry Andhra University, A.P.

** Professor, Management Studies SMIT, Bejupatnayak University, Orissa, Ankushpur, Berhampur, Orissa

7. Compensation, Rewards and Benefits Management;
8. Training and Development (Learning Management).

Implementation of such policies, processes or standards may be directly managed by the HR function itself, or the function may indirectly supervise the implementation of such activities by managers, other business functions or via third-party external partner organizations.

Human Resources Management Trends and Influences

In organizations, it is important to determine both current and future organizational requirements for both core employees and the contingent workforce in terms of their skills/technical abilities, competencies, flexibility etc. The analysis requires consideration of the internal and external factors that can have an effect on the resourcing, a development, motivation and retention of employees and other workers. The external factors are those largely out-with the control of the organization and include issues such as the economic climate, current and future trends of the labour market e.g. skills, education level, government investment into industries etc. On the other hand internal influences are broadly within the control of the organization to predict determine and monitor, for example the organizational culture underpinned by management behaviours (or style), environmental climate and the approach to ethical and corporate social responsibilities.

Major Trends

In order to know the business environment in which any organization operates, three major trends should be considered:

Demographics

the characteristics of a population/workforce, for example, age, gender or social class. This type of trend may have an effect in relation to pension offerings, insurance packages etc.

Diversity

the variation within the population/workplace. Changes in society now mean that a larger proportion of organizations are made up of 'baby-boomers' or older employees in comparison to thirty years ago. Advocates of 'workplace diversity' simply advocate an employee base that is a mirror reflection of the make-up of society insofar as race, gender, sexual orientation, etc.

Skills and qualifications

as industries move from manual to a more managerial professions so does the need for more highly skilled graduates. If the market is 'tight' (i.e. not enough staff for the jobs), employers will have to compete for employees by offering financial rewards, community investment, etc.

Human resources is a term used to describe the individuals who comprise the workforce of an organization, although it is also applied in labour economics to, for example, business sectors or even whole nations. Human resources is also the name of the function within an organization charged with the overall responsibility for implementing strategies and policies relating to the management of individuals (i.e. the human resources). This function title is often abbreviated to the initials 'HR'.

Human resources is a relatively modern management term having been coined in the 1960s. The origins of the function arose in those organisations which introduced 'welfare management' practices and also in those that adopted the principles of 'scientific management'. From these terms emerged a largely administrative management activity, co-ordinating a range of worker related processes and becoming known, in time as the 'personnel function'. Human resources progressively became the more usual name for this function, in the first instance in the United States as well as multinational corporations, reflecting the adoption of a more quantitative as well as strategic approach to workforce management, demanded by corporate management and the greater competitiveness for limited and highly skilled workers.

Background

The use of the term, 'human resources' by organizations to describe the workforce capacity available to devote to the achievement of its strategies has drawn upon concepts developed in Industrial/Organizational Psychology and System Theory. Human resources has at least two related interpretations depending on context. The original usage derives from political economy and economics, where it was traditionally called labour, one of four factors of production although this perspective has shifted as a consequence of further ongoing research into more strategic approaches. This first usage is used more in terms of 'human resources development' of the individuals within an organization, although the approach can also be applied beyond the level of the organization to that of industry sectors and nations.

The early development of the function can be traced back to at least two distinct movements. One element has its origins in the late 19th century, where organisations such as Cadburys at its Bournville factory recognised the importance of looking after the welfare of the workforce, and their families. The employment of women in factories in the United Kingdom during the First World War lead to the introduction of 'Welfare Officers'. Meanwhile, in the United States the concept of human resources developed as a reaction to the efficiency focus of Taylorism or 'scientific management' in the early 1900s which was developed as a response to the demand for ever more efficient working practices within highly mechanised factories, such as those of the Ford Motor Company. By 1920, psychologists and employment experts in the United States started the human relations movement, which viewed workers in terms of their psychology and fit with companies, rather than as interchangeable parts.

During the middle of the last century, larger corporations, typically those in the United States which had emerged after the Second World War recruited personnel from the US Military and were able to apply new selection, training, leadership and management development techniques, originally developed by the Armed Services working with for example, university-based occupational psychologists. Similarly, some leading European multinationals, such as Shell and Phillips had developed new approaches to personnel development and also drew on similar approaches already in use by Civil Service training establishments. Gradually, this resulted in the general spread of more sophisticated policies and processes requiring more centralised management via a Personnel Department comprising a range of both specialists and generalist teams.

The role of what would become more universally known as Human Resources grew throughout the middle of the 20th century. Tensions remained between academics placing emphasis either on what became known as 'Soft' or 'Hard' HR. Those professing so called 'soft HR' stressing the importance of such areas as leadership, cohesion, and loyalty which played important roles in organizational success. Meanwhile those promoting 'hard HR' continued to champion the advantage the more quantitatively rigorous and less 'soft' management techniques of the 1960s.

In the later part of the last century, both the title and traditional role of the personnel function was progressively being superseded with the emergence, in larger organizations at least, of so called strategic human resources management and the development of sophisticated human resources departments. Initially this may have involved little more than a renaming of the function, but where a transformation has occurred it has become distinguished by the Human Resources function also having a much more significant influence on the strategic direction of the organisation and becoming positioned in the organization, with designated board level representation.

Human Resources Purpose and Role

In the simplest terms, the objective of an organization's human resource management strategy is to maximize the return on investment from the organization's human capital and minimize financial risk. Human Resources seeks to achieve this by aligning the supply of skilled and qualified individuals, and the capabilities of the current workforce, with the ongoing and future business plans and requirements of the organization in order to maximise return on investment and seeks to secure the future survival and success of the entity. In ensuring such objectives are achieved, the human resource function purpose in this context is to implement the organisation's human resource requirements effectively but also pragmatically, taking account of legal, ethical and as far as is practical in a manner which retains the support and respect of the workforce.

Individual Responses

In regard to how individuals respond to the changes in a labour market the following should be understood:

Geographical spread

how far is the job from the individual? The distance to travel to work should be in line with the pay offered by the organization and the transportation and infrastructure of the area will also be an influencing factor in deciding who will apply for a post.

Occupational structure

the norms and values of the different careers within an organization. Mahoney 1989 developed 3 different types of occupational structure namely craft (loyalty to the profession), organization career (promotion through the firm) and unstructured (lower/unskilled workers who work when needed).

Generational difference

different age categories of employees have certain characteristics, for example their behaviour and their expectations of the organization.

Framework

Human Resources Development is a framework for the expansion of human capital within an organization or (in new approaches) a municipality, region, or nation. Human Resources Development is a combination of training and education, in a broad context of adequate health and employment policies, that ensures the continual improvement and growth of both the individual, the organization, and the national human resourcefulness. Adam Smith states, "The capacities of individuals depended on their access to education". Human Resources Development is the medium that drives the process between training and learning in a broadly fostering environment. Human Resources Development is not a defined object, but a series of organised processes, "with a specific learning objective" (Nadler,1984) Within a national context, it becomes a strategic approach to intersectoral linkages between health, education and employment.

Structure

Human Resources Development is the structure that allows for individual development, potentially satisfying the organization's, or the nation's goals. The development of the individual will benefit both the individual, the organization, or the nation and its citizens. In the corporate vision, the Human Resources Development framework views employees, as an asset to the enterprise whose value will be enhanced by development, "Its primary focus is on growth and employee development...it emphasises developing individual potential and skills" (Elwood, Olton and Trott 1996). Human Resources

Development in this treatment can be in-room group training, tertiary or vocational courses or mentoring and coaching by senior employees with the aim for a desired outcome that will develop the individual's performance. At the level of a national strategy, it can be a broad intersectoral approach to fostering creative contributions to national productivity.

Training

At the organizational level, a successful Human Resources Development programme will prepare the individual to undertake a higher level of work, "organized learning over a given period of time, to provide the possibility of performance change" (Nadler 1984). In these settings, Human Resources Development is the framework that focuses on the organizations competencies at the first stage, training, and then developing the employee, through education, to satisfy the organizations long-term needs and the individuals' career goals and employee value to their present and future employers.

Human Resources Development can be defined simply as developing the most important section of any business its human resource by, "attaining or upgrading the skills and attitudes of employees at all levels in order to maximise the effectiveness of the enterprise" (Kelly 2001). The people within an organization are its human resource. Human Resources Development from a business perspective is not entirely focussed on the individual's growth and development, "development occurs to enhance the organization's value, not solely for individual improvement. Individual education and development is a tool and a means to an end, not the end goal itself'. (Elwood F. Holton II, James W. Trott Jr). The broader concept of national and more strategic attention to the development of human resources is beginning to emerge as newly independent countries face strong competition for their skilled professionals and the accompanying brain-drain of their experience.

Recruitment

Employee recruitment forms a major part of an organization's overall resourcing strategies which seek to identify and secure the people needed for the organization to survive and succeed in the short to medium-term. Recruitment activities need to be responsive to the ever-increasingly competitive market to secure suitably qualified and capable recruits at all levels. To be effective these initiatives need to include how and when to source the best recruits internally or externally. Common to the success of either are; well-defined organizational structures with sound job design, robust task and .person specification and versatile selection processes, reward, employment relations and human resource policies, underpinned by a commitment for strong employer branding and employee engagement strategies.

Internal recruitment can provide the most cost-effective source for recruits if the potential of the existing pool of employees has been enhanced through training, development and other performance-enhancing activities such as performance appraisal, succession planning and development centres to review performance and assess employee development needs and promotional potential.

Increasingly, securing the best quality candidates for almost all organizations will rely, at least occasionally if not substantially, on external recruitment methods. Rapid changing business models demand skills of experiences which cannot be sourced or rapidly enough developed from the existing employee base. It would be unusual for an organization today to undertake all aspects of the recruitment process without support from third-party dedicated recruitment firms.

This may involve a range of support services, such as; provision of CVs or resumes, identifying recruitment media, advertisement design and media placement for job vacancies, candidate response handling, shortlisting, conducting aptitude testing, preliminary interviews or reference and qualification verification. Typically, small organizations may not have in-house resources or, in common with larger organizations, may not possess the particular skill-set required to undertake a specific recruitment assignment. Where requirements arise these will be referred on an ad hoc basis to government job centres or commercially run employment agencies.

Except in sectors where high-volume recruitment is the norm, an organization faced with an unexpected requirement for an unusually large number of new recruits at short notice will often hand over the task to a specialist external recruiter to manage the end-to-end resourcing programme. Sourcing executive-level and senior management as well as the acquisition of scarce or 'high-potential' recruits has been a long-established market serviced by a wide range of 'search and selection' or 'headhunting' consultancies which typically form long-standing relationships with their client organizations. Finally, certain organizations with sophisticated HR practices have identified there is a strategic advantage in outsourcing complete responsibility for all workforce procurement to one or more third-party recruitment agencies or consultancies. In the most sophisticated of these arrangements the external recruitment services provider may not only physically locate, or 'embed', their resourcing team(s) within the client organization's offices but will work in tandem with the senior human resource management team in developing the longer-term HR resourcing strategy and plan.

Other Considerations

Despite its more everyday use terms such as 'human resources' and similarly 'human capital' continue to be perceived negatively and maybe considered an insulting of people. They create the impression that people are merely commodities, like office machines or vehicles, despite assurances to the contrary Modern analysis emphasizes that human beings are not 'commodities' or 'resources', but are creative and social beings in a productive enterprise. The 2000 revision of ISO 9001 in contrast requires identifying the processes, their sequence and interaction, and to define and communicate responsibilities and authorities. In general, heavily unionised nations such as France and Germany have adopted and encouraged such approaches.

The International Labour Organization also in 2001 decided to revisit, and revise its 1975 Recommendation 150 on Human Resources Development. One view of these trends is that a strong social consensus on political economy and a good social welfare system facilitates labor mobility and tends to make the entire economy more productive, as labour can develop skills and experience in various ways, and move from one enterprise to another with little controversy or difficulty in adapting. Another view is that governments should become more aware of their national role in facilitating human resources development across all sectors.

Transnational Labour Mobility

An important controversy regarding labour mobility illustrates the broader philosophical issue with usage of the phrase 'human resources': governments of developing nations often regard developed nations that encourage immigration or 'guest workers' as appropriating human capital that is more rightfully part of the developing nation and required to further its economic growth.

Over time the United Nations have come to more generally support the developing nations' point of view, and have requested significant offsetting 'foreign aid' contributions so that a developing nation losing human capital does not lose the capacity to continue to train new people in trades, professions, and the arts.

Ethical Management

In the very narrow context of corporate 'human resources' management, there is a contrasting pull to reflect and require workplace diversity that echoes the diversity of a global customer base. Foreign language and culture skills, ingenuity, humour, and careful listening, are examples of traits that such programmes typically require. It would appear that these evidence a general shift through the human capital point of view to an acknowledgment that human beings do contribute much more to a productive enterprise than 'work': they bring their character, their ethics, their creativity, their social connections, and in some cases even their pets and children, and alter the character of a workplace. The term corporate culture is used to characterize such processes at the organizational level.

International HRM

International HRM places greater emphasis on a number of responsibilities and functions such as relocation, orientation and translation services to help employees adapt to a new and different environment outside their own country.

- Selection of employees requires careful evaluation of the personal characteristics of the candidate and his/her spouse.
- Training and development extends beyond information and orientation training to include sensitivity training and field experiences that will enable the manager to understand cultural differences better. Managers need to be protected from career development risks, re-entry problems and culture shock.
- To balance the pros and cons of home country and host country evaluations, performance evaluations should combine the two sources of appraisal information.
- Compensation systems should support the overall strategic intent of the organization but should be customized for local conditions.
- In many European countries—Germany for one, law establishes representation. Organizations typically

negotiate the agreement with the unions at a national level. In Europe it is more likely for salaried employees and managers to be unionized.

HR Managers should do the following things to ensure success

- Use workforce skills and abilities in order to exploit environmental opportunities and neutralize threats.
- Employ innovative reward plans that recognize employee contributions and grant enhancements.
- Indulge in continuous quality improvement through TQM and HR contributions like training, development, counseling, etc
- Utilize people with distinctive capabilities to create unsurpassed competence in an area, e.g. Xerox in photocopiers, 3M in adhesives, Telco in trucks etc.
- Decentralize operations and rely on self-managed teams to deliver goods in difficult times e.g. Motorola is famous for short product development cycles. It has quickly commercialized ideas from its research labs.
- Lay off workers in a smooth way explaining facts to unions, workers and other affected groups e.g. IBM, Kodak, Xerox, etc.

HR Managers today are focussing attention on the following

(a) Policies—HR policies based on trust, openness, equity and consensus.

(b) Motivation—Create conditions in which people are willing to work with zeal, initiative and enthusiasm; make people feel like winners.

(c) Relations—Fair treatment of people and prompt redress of grievances would pave the way for healthy work-place relations.

(d) Change agent—Prepare workers to accept technological changes by clarifying doubts.

(e) Quality Consciousness—Commitment to quality in all aspects of personnel administration will ensure success.

Due to the new trends in HR, in a nutshell the HR manager should treat people as resources, reward them equitably, and integrate their aspirations with corporate goals through suitable HR policies.

REFERENCES

a b Armstrong, Michael (2006). *A Handbook of Human Resource Management Practice* (10th ed.). London: Kogan Page. ISBN 0-7494-4631-5. OCLC 62282248.

"Personnel Management". *The Columbia Encyclopaedia* (Sixth Edition ed.). Columbia University Press. 2005. http://www. bartleby. com/ 65/x-/X-personne. html. Retrieved 2007-10-17. "Personnel Management—See Industrial Management".

Encyclopaedia Britannica (kl ed.). "Personnel Administration is also frequently called Personnel Management, Industrial Relations, Employee Relations".

Encyclopaedia Britannica.

Towers, David. "Human Resource Management Essays". http:// www.towers.fr/essays/hrm.html. Retrieved 2007-10-17.

Ulrich, Dave (1996). *Human Resource Champions. The next agenda for adding value and delivering results.* Boston, Mass.: Harvard Business School Press. ISBN 0-87584-719-6. OCLC 34704904.

Smit, Martin E.J.H. (2006). *HR, Show Me the Money; Presenting an Exploratory Model That Can Measure If HR Adds Value.*

The Strategic Impact of High Performance Work Systems

"About Cornell ILR". Cornell University School of Industrial and Labour Relations. http://www.ilr.cornell.edu/about/. Retrieved 23 August 2009.

Wilkinson, A. (1988). "Empowerment: Theory and Practice". *Personnel Review* 27 (1): 40-56. doi: 10.1108/00483489810368549. http:// hermia. emeraldinsight. com/vl=2601464/cl=84/nw= l/fm=docpdf/ rpsv/cw/mcb/00483486/v27nl/s3/p40. Retrieved 2007-10-17.

Legge, Karen (2004). *Human Resource Management: Rhetorics and Realities* (Anniversary ed.). Basingstoke: Palgrave Macmillan. ISBN .1-403-123600-5. OCLC 56730524.

Re-engineering Change in Higher Education

—G. Chandrayya*

Introduction

Expansion of higher education has led to a need for improved efficiency in administrative services, along with a greater range and flexibility in degree programmes than currently exists: new organisational structures are required (Ford *et al.*, 1996). A number of UK HEIs are currently attempting to use Business Process Re-engineering (BPR) as a change management strategy to obtain improvements in service. BPR arose at the beginning of the 1990s following attempts by large US companies to use Information Technology (IT), for linking business processes that cut across functional boundaries (Hammer and Champy, 1993). The aim was to secure competitive advantage. Penrod and Dolence(1992) view re-engineering as a suitable means for ensuring HEIs adapt to

* Senior Faculty Department of Commerce Govt. College(A), Rajahmundry, Andhra University, A.P.

the changing demands being placed upon them. However, as with other managerial imports from the private sector, there is some question over whether BPR can be applied to a public sector setting. Following many failures, BPR is no longer a term that inspires confidence in the private sector (Martinsons and Revenaugh, 1997). One of the main reasons for this high failure rate is thought to be BPR's failure to successfully manage the change of people (Davenport, 1995). In common with other public sector institutions, Higher Education Institutions (HEIs) have a number of strong interest groups that make achieving change a complex task. Thus, there is likely to be an even greater resistance in HEIs to change than in private sector companies. Attaining agreement on how processes should be redesigned is likely to be problematic.

The aim of this paper is to examine the applicability of BPR to Higher Education Institutions (HEIs) and, particularly, to determine how the 'people' element of re-engineering projects in HEIs effects the success of such projects. The performance of higher education is of great significance for the competitiveness of nations (Porter, 1990). It follows, therefore, that achieving successful change in HEIs is of the utmost importance, and determining the applicability of BPR to universities is a highly significant exercise. If 'traditional' working practices are no longer efficient in the modern university, then HEIs must determine effective ways of successfully achieving change. The experience with BPR in the private sector. has demonstrated that failing to change people has been a major barrier to success.

There are differing definitions of what BPR constitutes, but this paper does not aim to offer a precise definition of BPR: the concern is to examine HEIs where process-orientated change initiatives are taking place. A number of case studies have been constructed to analyse the applicability of BPR to HEIs, focussing on the extent to which organisational culture challenges successful implementation. This research started with a broad research question: How does organisational culture in HEIs impact on the implementation of BPR programmes?

Research Design

Appropriate selection of a research method was a key issue at the outset of the dissertation. This enabled worthwhile data to be collected from a number of HEIs carrying out BPR projects; it also ensured that subsequent analysis of the data produced valuable conclusions. Yin (1994) advocates a case-study approach for research that is concerned with addressing 'how' and 'why' type questions. This approach involves empirical enquiry that investigates a contemporary phenomenon in its real life context (Rose, 1991). Case-study research is therefore an appropriate strategy, as it examines how BPR programmes in HEIs are effected by organisational culture and resistance to change from within the organisation. Case studies are formed by collecting data which represents an interpretation of the research subjects' experiences, opinions and attitudes (McCormack Steinmetz, 1991). The case studies for this research are based mainly on the interview accounts of project stakeholders in universities undergoing BPR programmes. Seven interviews were carried out at five Universities. The interviews were semi-structured, and based on an interview schedule. The questions actually used in the interviews changed in the interview process, but usage of a schedule helped ensure all key areas of the topic were covered (McCormack Steinmetz, 1991).

Pressure for Change and BPR

In common with other public sector institutions, Higher Education Institutions (HEIs) are seeking to maintain the three 'Es' of efficiency, effectiveness and economy, by adopting private sector managerial techniques (Dobson and McNay, 1996). Business Process Re-engineering is currently been used as a change management strategy in a number of UK HEIs. A number of interrelated pressures have created the need for change in UK HEIs: expansion of higher education; changing student profile; pressures from industry; increased competition; information technology (IT) capability (Armstrong *et al*, 1997; Ford *et al*, 1996; Slowey, 1995).

The UK now has a mass system of higher education. The 1990s has seen the number of universities double; student numbers have quadrupled over the last 30 years (Scott, 1995). Thus the traditional structure of higher education, with an emphasis on staff-student contact is no longer adequate: There are not enough lecturers, library books or rooms, and there is not enough time...we have no choice but to do things differently' (Ford, *et al*, 1996: 17). New organisational structures are required to support new learning processes.

Despite the great potential for use of IT in higher education, it is not a common feature of teaching and learning in most institutions (Hall and White, 1997). This is a further pressure for change as HEIs must take advantage of IT developments to improve course delivery and reduce costs. Hicks (1997) views the present higher education system as being too fragmented, wasteful and inefficient. It is characterised by too many students participating in the same activities (e.g. lectures) at the same time: within a HEI there are students on different degree programmes covering the same materials in different locations. Exchange of information is not sufficiently exercised in HEIs: this can be seen as a major inefficiency (Tann, 1995). One of the advantages of multi-media resource-based learning, is the reusability of resources: students from different degree programmes—even different institutions—can access the same information as and when required (Hall and White, 1997). Increasing resource-based learning would result in fewer lectures, whilst the remaining lectures could be enhanced by computer technology (Barker, 1997). Hicks (1997) comments that most studies of computer based learning demonstrate its greater cost effectiveness by comparison to conventional learning. Taken to its extreme, multimedia resource-based learning results in the 'virtual university', an 'institution' not bound by the constraints of physical boundaries and accessible anywhere, anytime (Hansen and Lombardo, 1997).

Re-engineering HEIs

Business Process Re-engineering (BPR) has been identified in some quarters as a means by which universities can meet these pressures for change, utilising IT to increase efficiency and effectiveness (Penrod and Dolence, 1992; Dougherty, 1994; Casey, 1995). Ford *et al.* (1996) argue that BPR could enable HEIs to develop organisational structures that enable innovative teaching and learning methods, whilst maintaining some element of the important student-teacher relationship. For Penrod and Dolence (1992), BPR has significant potential for re-engineering the administrative functions of universities and ensuring control of higher education's costs.

BPR involves identification of the key business objectives of the organisation, and ensuring effective attainment of these objectives by redesigning business processes. Instead of the rigid functional boundaries represented by say, a 'sales department' and a 'purchasing department', roles and tasks are grouped around key business processes. Hicks (1997) considers that in the current situation, HEI departments work primarily on an independent basis. Arguments for re-engineering HEIs, advocate the establishment of institution-wide processes and dependencies across departmental boundaries. This can mean totally obliterating processes and starting over again, moving away from outdated and inefficient processes (Hammer, 1990). The motivation for this is the application of technology in organisations was often more to do with automating existing processes, what can be described as automating 'the existing mess'. Most work flows and job descriptions were developed before computers were introduced into organisations; processes have evolved rather than been designed (Hammer and Champy, 1993). Thus, for advocates of BPR, there is no rational justification for the retention of established processes in the modern organisation. Martinsons and Revenaugh (1997) comment that BPR has the potential to focus the re-engineered organisation's efforts on value-adding tasks, and reduce the number of workers required to perform a task. The processes that are re-engineered must be core processes, vital to the business, or initiatives will have little impact on overall performance (Thackray, 1993). If a core business element of an HEI is effective student learning (Eastcott & Farmer, 1996), then a BPR initiative would attempt to utilise IT to link teaching and learning processes across the functional boundaries of academic departments.

A crucial component required for the establishment of institution wide processes and dependencies in a University, is the introduction of an integrated IT infrastructure (Penrod and Dolence, 1992). This enables information to be transferred and accessed throughout the organisation and information becomes an institution-wide resource: '...it is exactly this enabling infrastructure that facilitates and helps drive the process of redesigning processes and procedures of the institution.' (Penrod 85 Dolence, 1992: 20). An institution-wide IT strategy leads to effective networking of voice, data and video; these are accessed regionally, nationally and even internationally. Buchanan and Gibb (1998) consider information to be a resource, that generates the knowledge required to achieve the goals and objectives of the modern organisation. For this reason, information can be regarded as a key source of competitive advantage (Ross *et al*, 1996). Penrod and Dolence argue that re-engineering is a means for achieving competitive advantage through effective management of information: 'Re-engineering is needed for business, industry, government, and educational enterprises to successfully move into the information/service economy' (1992: 1). At present, universities tend to be fragmented so that information is restricted to individual academics and departments. Ford *et al.* argue that if the challenge is to develop new and more appropriate learning environments then: 'this demands a new approach to course design and information management which cannot successfully be achieved without establishing new business processes' (1996: 32).

Re-engineering strives to counter poor responsiveness to customer needs (Willmott, 1994). Berry *et al.* (1990) point to the fact that customers are the real judges of service quality, but that this is not reflected in management decision making. Value is added when an organisation's activities are shaped to directly meet customer demands. For instance, the intention when re-engineering administrative processes in HEIs, is to make processes more student centred: processes should exist to meet students' needs (Penrod and Dolence, 1992). Successful BPR requires that processes are broadly defined in terms of customer (or cost) value, to improve performance across the entire business unit (Hall *et al.*, 1993). Kirkham (1996) stresses the importance of the diagnostic phase for determining processes to be re-engineered. In HEIs, the diagnostic phase would involve surveying both employees (academics, support staff) and customers (students) regarding their opinions on the services provided by the university. Above all, diagnosis is used to identify customers' service expectations (Berry *et al.*, 1990).

Re-engineering results in a workforce characterised by teams of multi-skilled flexible individuals, empowered by technological innovation. (Hammer and Champy, 1993). Bureaucratic delays are wiped out as employees in re-engineered organisations are empowered to contact sources of knowledge direct, side-stepping several tiers of management to complete what may previously have been a long cumbersome process in minutes. Empowerment is an important feature of BPR (Penrod and Dolence, 1992). Employees are held accountable for the success of the organisation; empowerment means that individual efforts can contribute directly to organisational success. As re-engineered jobs are organised around outcomes, employees perform all steps in a process rather than just a list of tasks.

Implementing a BPR project is far from a straightforward activity. It has not exactly been an unqualified success in the private sector, where following many failures it is now a widely derided practice (Martinsons and Revenaugh, 1997). Grint (1995) comments that 70 per cent of BPR programmes fail. A main reason for this high failure rate is thought to be BPR's failure to successfully take account of people in the re-engineering of processes: treating these people as 'bits and bytes' to be re-engineered (Davenport, 1995). According to Willmott (1995), the rhetoric surrounding BPR is powerful, confident and persuasive, but its computer science and engineering roots lead to it having a limited appreciation of the human dimension of organisational change. Geus's (1997) research into long standing successful private sector companies, reveals their success has been built on a recognition that people are an organisation's main asset. These long standing companies have a 'sense of community': if the community 'dies' then so does the business. People are seen as more important than production. BPR tends to counter years of employee commitment when processes are radically revised. Willmott (1994) argues that employees are assumed by BPR to be easily adjusted to fit new processes. If employee resistance occurs, it represents inertia and can be dealt with provided that senior management are sufficiently persuasive. BPR fails to take account of the fact that employee objections might be legitimate. HEIs now have strategic plans which might be seen as useful for formulating BPR initiatives. However, a university is a highly complex organisation where there are many different ideas about what the university is trying to achieve (Taylor, 1995). Taylor comments that the situation is less problematic in companies, where the executive define the mission and everyone is expected to work towards that mission. The mission of HEIs is complicated by a tradition of academic freedom in which individual academics develop autonomously; management style tends towards administrative rather than proactive leadership (Thorley, 1995). Academic freedom has been somewhat countered in the 1990s, in that academics are subject to an increasing number of accountability mechanisms, such as Teaching Quality assessments (Hodges, 1998). Nonetheless, despite these increasing constraints, BPR initiatives in higher education will face a culture of individualism in higher education; any BPR project will have to overcome this problem (Hall 85 White, 1997). The concern might be that staff feel demoralised at the loss of 'academic freedom', creating an atmosphere that is not conducive to innovation and improved performance (Kirkham, 1996). Change in Higher Education has tended to restrict academic freedom, so further radical change is unlikely to be welcomed (Palfreyman & Warner, 1996). For instance, at the University of East Anglia some faculty perceived the introduction of modular courses and semesters as restrictive, rather than a means for providing students with greater flexibility (the intended purpose) (Rich and Scott, 1997). Academics will also be concerned that re-engineering is a threat to their professional status, as their role might change to that of managing and building learning resources (House and Watson, 1995). Empowerment might be emphasised as a major feature of BPR, but re-engineering programmes tend to be very authoritarian (Thackray, 1993). Leaders of change are required to dictate where the organisation is going for the change strategy to be successful—even though the organisation's employees find the process of change unacceptable. Strategic change must therefore take account of organisational culture (DeLisi, 1990). Re-engineering can be criticised for failing to adequately link organisational culture with business culture. Culture is often defined as 'the way we do things around here' (Dobson and McNay, 1996). This might seem a straightforward notion, but it hides an underlying complexity and significance that must be attributed to organisational culture (Heracleous, 1995). According to Johnson (1992), the culture of an organisation is represented by a 'paradigm', which is the core set of beliefs and attitudes held by employees. The paradigm develops throughout the history of the organisation, and is shared to varying degrees by members of the organisation. Current processes and roles are inextricably linked with the paradigm: 'it lies within a cultural web which bonds it to the action of organizational life.' (Johnson, 1992: 30). Effective organisational change is therefore likely to be achieved when it is in line with the organisational paradigm and the cultural, social and political norms of organisational life.

The problems begin when radical change—such as that associated with BPR—attempts to take people away from the 'core beliefs': 'the way we do things around here'. Thus incremental change is more likely to succeed as it entails minimal disruption to the paradigm. This seems to be particularly the case in HEIs where successful change tends to be of an organic nature: it does not go against the grain (Elton, 1997).

Achieving a situation where academic and support staff are in agreement with change is a far from easy task. However: 'Managing change successfully, ultimately depends upon understood and shared values and objectives, for the managers and the managed.'(House 85 Watson, 1995: 19). Slee (1995) describes the implementation of a Total Quality Management (TQM) initiative in his department (at the University of Durham), as succeeding because the philosophy underpinning the approach was in tune with the existing staff value system. This was implemented in a single department; institution-wide change is likely to involve negotiating a wider range of mindsets. However, achieving change across an entire HEI depends on an ability to establish consensus quickly (Rich & Scott, 1997). The need for consensus could be a major barrier for utilising BPR in HEIs, particularly if the aim is to achieve radical change.

Hall and White (1997) argue that the technological barriers associated with computer based learning—such as operating across different hardware platforms—are far easier to overcome than the cultural issues in HEIs. For instance, academics seek to put their own spin on learning. As Davenport (1995) comments, IT is useful when it helps people to work, but simply ploughing resources into technology and not working with people to develop its use has a negative impact. Innovations such as the Virtual laboratory' which simulate 'real-life' science experiments, could play a crucial role in the re-engineered HEI: providing access to learning any time, any place, at a reduced cost. However, the challenge is to achieve a balance between computer and real-life (Hicks, 1997). Organisational culture can be an instrument of competitive advantage (Willmott, 1993). From this viewpoint, the fact that the culture of universities emphasises the human element is a source of advantage. Strengthening this culture is a means for enhancing organisational performance, because it will secure greater commitment and flexibility from employees (Willmott, 1993). Brown (1997) argues that if the 'humanity' of HEIs is lost then they will not function: universities are essentially people-centred institutions.

The Research Environments

Five universities provided the focus for this research: they are anonymised in the following account of their characteristics. Midland University is a 50-year-old multi-campus University, with high ratings for both teaching and research. It has over 20,000 students and undergraduate places are highly sought after. The 'BPR initiative' is concerned with the improvement of administrative processes, identifying how efficiency gains could be made in administrative services by meeting the needs of the University's Schools. In the initial stages, the management group (led by the Vice Chancellor) appointed a team to evaluate administrative activities, and then recommend appropriate programmes for improvement. The team was introduced to BPR project management by a leading management consultancy. Consultation was undertaken at all levels of the organisation to enable evaluation of administrative processes.

Highland University was an early foundation and despite a history of change, retains some archaic characteristics. However, it is a very successful institution with high ratings for both teaching and research. Departments within the institution have a significant level of autonomy, which means change programmes have to secure the agreement of many factions: change purely from the top cannot be achieved under the current framework. A significant power is the senate which consists of 450 university members, compared to a senate of just 25 in Newcastle University (a comparable institution). A major component of the BPR project is a Student Information Project. Student information and degree regulations at Highland are highly complex. Consultation was undertaken throughout the various administrative services and with academic departments within the institution.

North Eastern University (NEU) is a centre of excellence in teaching and research. The University is based on two sites, with a main campus housing most academic departments and services. Changes have been occurring in this institution since the early 1990s, when in common with many other Universities, academic degree courses were restructured into modules and semesters. At the same time there were moves within the University to co-ordinate management and administrative computing. In 1994 NEU set up a Information Strategy Review Group (ISRG) which following analysis of the institution's activities, identified 12 major institution-wide processes (e.g.: 'managing the estate' and 'student course provision'). The ISRG focus has been on administrative processes, but the intention is to redirect activities to teaching and learning support: Web based teaching resources are being developed.

Yorkshire University, one of the largest civic Universities in the UK, has a commitment to promoting excellence whilst achieving and sustaining international standing in teaching, learning and research. Yorkshire is implementing a major, new MIS for finance, human resources pay roll and student administration. This represents a huge £4-5m systems investment for the University. As with North Eastern University, a major project concerns the devolution of control of systems to departmental level. Central administration will then be able to take on a more strategic, customer focussed role, monitoring trends and benchmarking administrative services against competitors: recognition that Higher Education is becoming an increasingly competitive market. This current initiative is not being given the BPR label, partly to avoid association with a previous, failed attempt at re-engineering administration. The new MIS will provide the tools that resource centres have been lacking to do an efficient management job. There has been considerable consultation with the main user groups to enable determination of system requirements. The Vice Chancellor has an active interest in the advancement of knowledge management, so there is a commitment from the top for strategic information systems development.

North Western University (NWU) has a more managerial ethos, with more hierarchical and centralised management structures than are present in longer established universities (Thorley, 1995). Despite top rated teaching in some departments, this HEI is having to negotiate a precarious financial situation. The Executive (Vice Chancellor, Provost, Bursar, Registrar) have given backing to a wholesale process redesign: change of a more radical nature than is displayed in the other case study sites is aimed for. Members of the Executive worked with some high level business consultants for a period of about three months on developing corporate strategy. A 'transformation report', recommending changes across the entire institution, has been prepared by a transformation design team. Currently a number of strategies can be identified; a coherent corporate strategy is not in existence. An integrated information system is an important component of change, as currently there are 17 officially recognised databases and many others are in existence, with all the related problems such as duplication being created as a result. The intention is to go back to basics and determine what actually needs to be done to complete a process, rather than simply seeking to improve current practices.

Factors Affecting the Change Process

Introduction

The BPR projects at the case study HEIs are still being implemented. For this reason, the interviews sought to examine the design of the projects, the challenges that project stakeholders are facing in the initial stages of project roll-out and anticipated problems. The discussion that follows, begins by identifying how projects are initiated and the wide consultation that goes on at the outset of the BPR programmes. A range of factors are then identified that make implementing BPR in these institutions a difficult proposition.

The cases are reviewed under the headings of: Project Intiaition, Wide Consultation, Senior Managment Approval, Complex Information Requirements, Insitutional Politics and Entrenched Values, Academic Freedom, Inertia, Business process improvement: 'conservative' change programmes, IT Driven Change, Mainting the Status Quo; Failure to 'Re-engineer' Human Resources, Organisational Transformation.

Project Initiation

The case studies demonstrate that the impetus for initiatives tends to come from senior management at the 'executive' level. Responsibility for the BPR programmes is then delegated to a lower tier of management. At Midland University, a project stake-holding team was appointed by the executive Steering Group for the project, consisting of a senior administrative manager from an academic department, a financial accounting manager from central administration, an information services manager representing the Library, an IT manager representing Computing Services and the Administrative Secretary. Similar teams were formed at the other case study institutions so as to represent the various functional areas within their HEI. Senior management at Midland set the parameters for change as being a commitment to identifying means for more effective and efficient management of administrative support processes.

At NWU the project parameters were broader to include possible redesign of teaching and learning processes. The purpose of establishing interdisciplinary teams to work on the projects is two-fold: first, the team members could take an overall perspective of their particular area; secondly, the members of the team would be able to consult widely with the various groups of people involved in the process, to gain a diagnosis of the situation.

Complex Information Requirements

The diagnostic processes carried out by each case study HEI, revealed that administrative support services draw on diverse sources of information, and that departments generally run their own independent databases in parallel to central databases. As a result, university information systems are fragmented. Systems are started off in the centre for purposes such as accounting: they do not necessarily meet departmental requirements. Differences between departments dictate that departments will manage their own data, for their own purposes. *Ad hoc* developments to central systems are undertaken in an attempt to meet these 'other' needs, but such uncoordinated practices lead to 'system mess'. For instance at NWU the existing Student Information System:

> *'grew up in bits, initially meeting the requirements of central Registry...then access was made available to other areas—but they didn't design or have input into it. You end up with a mess.' (Informant Interview, NWU).*

While the systems may be established to reflect the interests of one group of users, problems arise because Universities have a range of user groups with differing information requirements. A further significant problem is duplication, which is created by departments running their own systems along side central systems. As with Highland, where departments had been keeping exam results on departmental databases, printing these out and forwarding to central administration, who then had to re-type results into a central database. At NEU the Team Leader comments:

"...people in departments were constantly sending messages to the centre on bits of paper, e-mails and whatever" (Informant Interview, NEU).

Work is done more than once creating great inefficiencies. A BPR effort will face the difficulty of establishing an 'integrated' information system, within which data capture is undertaken at one point. Apart from the difficulty involved with determining diverse user information needs and meeting them all, the BPR initiative has to ensure that centralised systems are used. This is a question of providing different sections of the university with what they require. The change is related to culture in that it becomes necessary for departments to operate in a more uniform manner. However, attaining agreement on what a process should constitute is problematic. In the process evaluation at Midland University, financial process recommendations conflicted with those covered by student administration:

'The Student Administration project workers just went off and said, 'we're going to do all this (the recommendations) with the new student administration system we're developing, so lets just bear that in mind as we do that" (Informant Interview, NEU).

Any agenda for change in the complex HEI will struggle to achieve a coherent and co-ordinated set of recommendations. An informant at NWU commented:

"...we've got several rival administrative frameworks in the university and they are not working together" (Informant Interview, NWU).

Institutional Politics and Entrenched Values

The HEI case studies possess a significant (although varying) amount of 'historical baggage', so that working practices can be out-dated and fail to add value. Some roles exist purely to check the work of others. The process analysis at NEU revealed many Working committees' and different functional layers of responsibility for authorisation. Completion of administrative tasks was a complicated process, but various rubber stamping activities were found to be unnecessary obstacles to process completion. Johnson's (1992) organisational culture 'paradigm'—the core set of beliefs and attitudes held by employees ('the way we do things around here')—is demonstrated to be a powerful factor in the case study HEIs. The current processes and roles appear to be inextricably linked with the cultural paradigm: organisational structures and functions are entrenched in these institutions, and BPR is bound to conflict with a few traditions when it is introduced.

Dobson and McNay (1996) posit that many interest groups exist in HEIs; this is borne out by analysis of the case studies. 'Interest groups' of considerable strength are individual departments. The cultural paradigm is further complicated by the fact that individual departments often have their own cultures and operate on an autonomous basis. Slee (1995) considers that a TQM initiative in his department, succeeded because the philosophy underpinning the approach was in tune with the existing staff value system. It has to be noted that this was implemented within a single department; achieving alignment with the core beliefs and values of departments institution-wide is less feasible given the variation in cultures between departments. It is not simply a question of negotiating one organisational culture when implementing change: thereis a multiplicity of cultures. This was most apparent in the long-established Highland University, but also evident in the newer NWU. As a New University, NWU might be expected to have a more managerial structure than institutions such as Midland and Highland, but that has to be weighed against the 'polytechnic culture' which still influences NWU. The 'polytechnic culture' describes a series of independent Schools where different cultures apply.

An informant at NWU considers that managing the University's 15 Academic Schools as a single entity, is somewhat improbable given that there would be a 15-1 reporting relationship: each School is in possession of a powerful Head of School. In a large HEI such as Yorkshire, there is inevitably going to be a significant level of autonomy at the departmental level:

> *"You have to accept a quite significant degree of autonomy...they have legitimate reasons in many cases for doing things differently" (Informant Interview, Yorkshire).*

For instance, Medical Schools have complicated funding relationships with the NHS. Academic schools were described in different institutions variously as 'fiefdoms' (Highland), 'cottage industries' (Midland) and Independent islands' (NWU).

At Midland, there is a binary system of reporting so that managers have control over a specific function (e.g, Bursar - Finance). An informant from Midland doubts the logic of this: research is a core area of Midland's business yet it is split under the control of two functions. This informant argues that it would make more sense to have a Director of Research to co-ordinate all research administration activities. A BPR programme strives to achieve such streamlining of activities, but it would involve a major restructuring, something unlikely to receive the necessary backing given that it threatens the roles of those it needs to have support from. As Willmott (1995) would put it: turkeys do not vote for Christmas.

Organisational Transformation

NWU are rather more radical at the outset of their initiative, constructing a broad agenda for organisational change through BPR. Organisational cultural factors experienced in the other universities, such as academic freedom, and a decentralised management structure, are still significant factors for those implementing process review in this institution. The fact that this HEI aims for change of a radical nature seems to be related to top management evaluation of the financial situation. This HEI is having to face up to significant financial problems: it has managed to budget for the next financial year, but then has to undergo significant cost-cutting initiatives. NWU's executive visited a number of US HEIs and discovered that BPR could be used to manage the effects of cost-cutting. The financial situation at NWU has opened the door for a radical re-engineering programme: executive backing is present (at least in the early stages of the project), and the teams charged with process review have a wide remit for change. The agenda for change is all encompassing, outlining how all arcas of the university could be transformed to advance organisational effectiveness. Determining precisely how change should be managed is another matter, although there is recognition of the limitations of an approach that involves tinkering with existing processes: new processes are to be implemented. An infomant at NWU stresses the necessity of going back to basics and determining what the 'root and branch' needs are for a process. There has been too much adding to what already exists and not removing redundant practices:

> *'People don't know why they are doing things—if you ask why they are doing something, you get some very funny answers...there is an awful lot of window-dressing'.*

Re-centralisation of systems is also seen as a necessary requirement, to achieve the necessary integration of information systems. For this to happen this informant was aware that a cultural change has to occur. Also, the information requirements of different sections are diverse, making integration a difficult proposition. Currently, bids to re-engineer administrative processes are the most developed, whilst plans to redesign learning and teaching are somewhat less clear. This is an indication of the difficulty associated with applying BPR to teaching and learning. At NWU, this informant takes the approach of modelling what the process in question would ideally look like, and then identifies how it could exist in the 'real world'. This represents a similar philosophy to that of Grint (1995) who considers BPR to be a Utopia to work towards, even though it is unlikely to be arrived at. A compromise has to be reached between the organisational circumstances in existence, such as cultural and political factors, and the process model. NWU has to negotiate a powerful academic management structure of departments who expect to manage themselves: consensus change is required. Thus there are significant problems faced in implementing BPR. However, having made the point about the necessity for achieving change through consensus, there is an element of urgency for NWU to change. This means that gradually attaining consensus over a long period of time is not a viable option. A different informant at NWU admits:

> *'I'm not sure that there will be en mass support (from academics), but this is where the Provost as academic leader of the institution has to come in. It can't evolve naturally just with those people who want to make it happen, it has to happen rather more quickly than that'.*

Whether or not full awareness of the fininacial situation will convince people that radical changes are appropriate is open to question. Certainly an element of top down direction will be necessary, but managing the tension this may create with the autonomous departments, is an important issue for consideration. The recommendations that have been made in the transformation report might demonstrate efficient managerial practice, but it could be that it is only awareness of the financial predicament that will provide the required impetus for change.

Conclusion

UK HEIs are under pressure to change. This pressure comes from a number of interrelated factors: the expansion of HE, a changing student profile, pressures from industry, increased competition and IT capability. All these factors seem to be driving HEIs seek managerial tools for maintaining efficiency, effectiveness and economy under new circumstances. Improvement of administrative, research, and teaching and learning activities are seen as essential. The case studies reveal that many of the HEIs have taken the view that before any redesign of teaching and learning can be considered inefficiencies in administrative management must be addressed. Process review teams at these institutions have identified that administrative information systems and processes in these HEIs are fragmented and inefficient. In the HEI environment, there is a necessity for both central and departmental databases. Departments tend to implement their own databases in parallel to central systems, in order to meet individual departmental requirements. However, as these departments are part of a single University, they have to have a link to central databases: this presents many opportunities for duplication of effort and work. Against this background, the five HEI case studies are attempting to utilise a form of process change in order to become more efficient. The aim is to become more process orientated and eliminate redundant, non-value adding practices; the appeal of BPR is its focus on utilising IT solutions to link business processes that cut across functional boundaries. BPR is seen as a means for addressing a situation where there might be around 50 departments, of which many function in different ways. Re-engineering could ensure that practices in these departments become more similar, and that departments work with an integrated information system.

Analysis of the interview data reveals what can best be described as 'business process improvement' rather than radical redesign of processes. Instead of total obliteration of existing processes, these institutions are focussing on improving administrative processes. Establishing a integrated information system is a major component of this, but the emphasis is on widening access to existing systems, modifying these slightly to meet individual departmental requirements: the initiatives are IT driven. It is not simply a question of building information systems on the basis of user (department) demands. The limited re-engineering aims are prompted by the restrictive factors that initiators of change must negotiate. Any re-engineering type programme implemented will be effected by the cultural, political and management structural factors it encounters in a HEI. In formulating the recommendations, the HEIs consult widely to gain a diagnosis of the current situation. Staff input is essential as change in Higher Education is attained through consensus. However, consensus is most likely to be gained if the recommendations are broadly in line with the existing cultural paradigm. Thus the recommendations reflect the conservative nature of departments within a HEI. Despite the fact that what is being implemented is not radical re-engineering, the projects face significant barriers to achieving change successfully. BPR techniques and tools might have something to offer these HEIs, in terms of the potential for creating a more efficient and coherent operation. However, that potential has to be matched against the cultural and structural factors within HEIs. Subsequently these factors are likely to further diminish the scope for change made in the recommendations stage, as the attempt is made to actually implement the project. NWU's BPR recommendations suggest a more radical approach, but there is recognition that the HEI environment of NWU might reduce the level of process change actually undertaken. There is a difference between how a process would ideally exist and how it will exist in the 'real world'. The intention might be to start completely anew, but the reality could represent building on past practices. The case studies demonstrate the unique characteristics present in the HE environment: autonomous, powerful departmental units and the notion of academic freedom. Departments tend to have considerable autonomy and operate in individualistic ways—partly because there may be practical reasons for them to do this, but also because through their history and development they have evolved in certain ways. Departments install their own databases because central databases tend not to suffice for individual needs. To a certain extent, differences will arise through practical reasons: for example Medical Schools have particular requirements relating to their close collaboration with the NHS. Beyond such legitimate' grounds for differentiation, these departments have developed different working practices and roles which are now established and entrenched. If process review reveals administrative functions to be overly complicated, with certain roles existing purely to check the work of others, then that does not mean removal of these is necessarily straightforward. HEIs have strong organisational cultures and the cultural paradigm is inextricably linked to existing practices and roles.

The problems faced when applying BPR techniques to administrative services are accentuated when applied to teaching and learning. With teaching and learning, any redesign faces less clear accountabilities than is the case with administration. The aims of administrative services are easier to identify than teaching and learning aims: the expected outcomes of the teaching and learning process are more debatable. Academic freedom is a hugely important issue when consideration is given to redesign of teaching and learning. Academics tend to expect a certain amount of freedom to pursue the teaching techniques they consider most appropriate for their field of expertise. When the case study HEIs are attempting to re-engineer teaching and learning it represents a limited form of change. The emphasis is on making learning support technology available to those academics that want it. This is a 'bottom-up' form of change in that it is down to the individual academic.to implement changes if they consider it will improve the teaching and learning process. Academic freedom is such a powerful notion within the HEIs that changing teaching and learning cannot be easily attained without support from individual academics.

Thus an institution wide initiative to redesign learning and teaching can only be a gradual, incremental process. The concern to maintain the essence of the academic's central role in teaching and learning provision means that innovations introduced are used to supplement conventional methods. At NWU the re-engineering of teaching is intended to be of a more radical nature. However, at the same time there is realisation that change must not detract from what academics do best' (e.g. providing lectures). The NWU project team acknowledge the importance of achieving change through consensus, but the urgency of the need for change—a precarious financial situation—means that more gradual and incremental redesign is inappropriate: a certain degree of top-down dictation is required. This is likely to prove a source of conflict given that change in Higher Education is usually by consensus.

To conclude, the case study HEIs are for the most part implementing change programmes that represent a fairly limited approximation of BPR techniques. These projects are not about radically changing the organisation by obliterating existing processes. Instead it is process improvement; more radical BPR projects will conflict with the organisational factors identified in this research. In particular the power of academic departments, the professional status of academics and inertia within the HEIs make radical re-engineering an unlikely proposition. The experiences of the case study HEIs suggest that incremental process change may succeed in achieving modest efficiency gains, particularly when applied to administrative services. Teaching and learning support requires an even greater emphasis on incremental change; it is down to the individual academic to implement any changes. However, the fact that these BPR projects are process and IT driven suggest dramatic service improvements will not be made: insufficient attention is given to the human resources side of change management.

REFERENCES

Armstrong, S., Thompson, G., Brown, S. (editors). (1997). *Facing up to Radical Change in Universities and Colleges.* London: Kogan Page.

Barker, P. (1997). 'Assessing Attitudes to Electronic Lectures'. In: Armstrong, S., Thompson, G., Brown, S. (editors). (1997). *Facing up to Radical Change in Universities and Colleges.* 9-17. London: Kogan Page.

Berry, V.L., Zeithaml, V.A., Parasuraman, A. (1990). 'Five Imperatives for Improving Service Quality', *Sloan Management Review,* Summer 1990, 29-38.

Brown, S. (1997). 'Facing up to Radical Changes In Universities and Colleges'. In: Armstrong, S., Thompson, G., Brown, S. (editors). *Facing up to Radical Change in Universities and Colleges.* 181-186. London: Kogan Page.

Bryman, A. (1988). *Quantity and Quality in Social Research.* London: Routledge.

Buchanan, S., Gibb, F. (1998). The Information Audit: An Integrated Strategic Approach', *International Journal of Information Management,* 1998, 18, 29-47.

Casey, J.M. (1995). 'A Strategic Business Improvement Model for Higher Education. Move Over TQM—Here Comes BPR', *Annual Conference of the South-eastern Regional Association of Physical Plant Administrators of Universities and Colleges,* Oct. 16, 1995 EDRS Conference Report.

Davenport, T.H. (1995). The Fad that Forgot People', *Fast Company,* November, 1995. http://www.fastcompany.com/online/01/reengin.html (29 December 2002).

DeLisi, P.S. (1990). 'Lessons from the Steel Axe: Culture, Technology and Organisational Change', *Sloan Management Review,* Fall 1990, 83-93.

Dobson, S., McNay, I. (1996). 'Organisational Culture'In: Warner, D., Palfeyman, D. (editors). *Higher Education Management—The Key Elements.* 16-32. Buckingham: SRHE/OU Press.

7

Business Process Re-engineering (B.P.R.) for Manufacturing Industries

—Dr. D. Tata Rao*
—Dr. R.N. Misra**

Summary

The Manufacturing Industry today is significantly challenged by slow growth and a tough global economy. In order to remain competitive in the global marketplace, manufacturers are adopting radical corporate strategies—like flattening the organization, globalizing production, forming strategic alliances with customers, suppliers and competitors, merging with other companies to form new structures, decentralizing business units, and creating global business units.

Having to deal with a whole new set of non-traditional competitors can slow progress of even the sleekest of companies. This has necessitated Business Process Re-Engineering (BPR) for

* Senior Lecturer in Commerce, Government Degree College, Yalamanchili, Visakhapatnam District.

** Professor of Management Studies, S.M.I.T. Biju Patnaik University, Berhampur, Orissa.

manufactuiers of all sizes today. BPR is being used as a vehicle for re-aligning strategy, operations and systems to deliver significantly increased financial results and customer satisfaction. It helps to find ways to do more with less and provide a better product or service in the minimum amount of time—speed, quality, and cost being the key drivers.

This paper provides a brief overview of BPR and its critical success factors, in addition to discussing applicability of BPR to the manufacturing industry, based on current trends and corporate strategies.

Introduction

The manufacturing industry is accelerating at a rapid pace today. Manufacturers are under tremendous pressure to develop more products at the lowest price, and market them to an international and increasingly demanding customer base. As a result, the successful principles earlier governing the industry—like specialization of labour, mass production, assembly lines bringing work to the worker, complex production, planning and scheduling systems, and hierarchical organization structure—have become inadequate to meet today's challenges. This is the effect of world becoming an increasingly competitive global environment of continuous and un-predictable changes.

> BPR is being used as a vehicle for re-aligning strategy, operations and systems to deliver significantly increased financial results and customer satisfaction.

With acceleration in the pace and magnitude of business pressure and changes, new and more effective approaches had to be adopted. As a result, companies competing in the global arena chose BPR, to re-structure their organizations and business processes to align with their new corporate strategic goals. The same has helped them to survive and sustain their competitive advantage.

The following section gives a brief overview of BPR—what is BPR, why BPR, the critical success factors of BPR, relationship between BPR, and a common methodology for BPR.

BPR—A Brief Overview

What is BPR?

Business Process Re-engineering is the critical analysis and radical redesign of existing business processes within and between organizations, to achieve breakthrough improvements in performance measures.

A business process is a set of logically related activities that take one or more kinds of input and create an output of value to the customer, it lays a strong emphasis on how work is done within an organization Business processes have two important characteristics—customers, and these customers cross organizational boundaries.

> BPR differs from TQM (Total Quality Movement) in that, BPR emphasis on radical changes over a bounded time frame (typically short), whereas TQM emphasizes on minor changes and refinements over an open ended period of time.

Processes are generally identified in terms of beginning and end points, interfaces, and organization units involved. Examples of processes include—developing a new product, ordering goods from a supplier, creating a marketing plan, etc.

BPR differs from TQM (Total Quality Movement) in that, BPR emphasis on radical changes over a bounded time frame (typically short), whereas TQM emphasizes on small changes/ refinements over an open ended period of time.

Why BPR?

Customers, competition and change are major sources of environmental pressure for a company. Today's customers know what they want, what they are willing to pay for, and how they can get products and services on their terms.

Competition, with respect to price, quality, selection, and promptness of delivery is continuously increasing Removal of trade barriers, increased international cooperation and the creation of technological innovation cause competition to intensify.

BPR Phases

- Develop Strategic Vision
- Identify and Select Business Process Reengineering Opportunities
- Analyze and Document Current Process(es)
- Benchmarking
- Identify IT Levers and Cost Performance

Change continues to occur—markets, products, services, technology, business environment and people keep changing frequently in an unpredictable and significant manner. BPR helps address these through:

- Increase in Process Efficiencies
- Improvement in Customer Service
- Cost Reduction
- Data and Information Sharing
- Use of IT—right place at the right time
- Reduce Duplicate, Stove-Pipe Systems
- Reuse Technology
- Leverage New Technologies as Key Change and Efficiency Enablers

What are the different phases of BPR?

There are several methodologies available for BPR—some advocate incremental changes, and some, radical. The best of breed approach would be a judicious mix of both radical and incremental changes—a decision driven by the strategic nature of business processes involved. All methodologies typically cover the following key phases:

- ***Develop Strategic Vision:*** BPR is driven by a business vision which implies specific business objectives such as Cost Reduction, Time Reduction, Output Quality improvement, and QWL/Learning/Empowerment
- ***Identify and Select Business Process Reengineering Opportunities:*** Most firms use the high-impact approach, which focuses on the most important processes or the ones that conflict greatly with the business vision. A lesser number of firms use the exhaustive approach, which attempts to identify all processes within an organization and then prioritize them in order of redesign urgency.
- ***Analyze and Document Current Process(es):*** This phase focuses on identifying and avoiding repetition of old mistakes, in addition to providing a baseline for future improvements. A thorough understanding of core business processes is the prime emphasis here.
- ***Benchmarking:*** Benchmarking covers a thorough analysis of the best practices used by competitors, and helps in understanding market dynamics.
- ***Identify IT Levers and Cost Performance Metrics:*** Awareness of IT capabilities can and should influence process design.
- ***Design New Process(es):*** The actual design does not imply end of the BPR process. It is to be viewed as a prototype, with successive iterations. The metaphor of prototype aligns the BPR approach with quick delivery of results, and the involvement and satisfaction of customers.
- ***Develop a Business Case for Alternatives Selection and Implementation:*** This should cover as is process

assessment, recommended alternate solutions and a thorough analysis of the costs and benefits associated with implementing the proposed solution, apart from assumptions and perceived risks.

- ***Formulate Implementation Plan and/or Pilot Programme***: This is to convince the management that the solution is actually implemented in a bounded time frame and should typically cover—implementation components, implementation timeline, major milestones and major dependencies.
- ***Review, Approval and Execution:*** Get approval from the board for execution.

BPR and IT

New technologies often provide breakthroughs in business process reengineering. They enable new processes that previously were not possible. The internet is an example of a technology that has fundamentally changed customer service processes by giving customers new ways to access information, conduct transactions and interact with companies. The personal computer, LAN/WAN, and scanners for barcodes have a similar impact Cellular telephony and wireless services are other examples.

> The ultimate success of BPR depends on the people who do it and on how well they can be motivated to be creative and to apply their detailed knowledge to the redesign of business processes.

Because of the breakthrough capability of new technology, reengineering teams need to invest time researching and assessing the potential applications of new tools, applications and systems. This research is unrestricted in scope, with the only limitations being good judgment of the technology team to investigate areas that have a reasonable chance of applying to the project.

IT and BPR have a recursive relationship. IT capabilities should support business processes, and business processes should be in terms of the capabilities IT can provide. IT and BPR have a recursive relationship. IT capabilities should support business processes, which should be in terms of the capabilities that IT can provide. Wipro has contributed significantly to its customers in both of these areas. This contribution can be attributed to:

- Wipro's technical consulting depth on a broad spectrum of products and technologies.
- Wipro's domain consulting depth, which has been acquired through successful end to end execution of large projects in key manufacturing domains like ERP, SCM, PLM, and so on.

What are the Critical Success Factors of BPR?

BPR is a non-trivial endeavor that manufacturers engage in to realize their strategic business vision. So there are important strategic dimensions to BPR—for example, developing and prioritizing key business objectives, defining the process structure and assumptions, identifying trade-offs between processes, identifying new product and market opportunities, coordinating the re-engineering effort, and developing a human resources strategy. The critical success factors for BPR can be summarized as follows:

- Senior Management Commitment and Sponsorship (Top-Down commitment)
- Realistic Expectations
- Empowered and Collaborative Workers (Bottom-up functional support)
- Strategic Context of Growth and Expansion
- Shared Vision
- Sound Management Practices

- Appropriate People Participating Full-time (Right resources)
- Change Tolerance
- Sufficient Budget

> Agility is achieved through regular business process re-engineering, and re-segmenting of business processes including the manufacturing processes into 'virtual' transient organizations or teams, having individual or small customer group aligned objectives.

The ultimate success of BPR depends on the people who do it and on how well they can be motivated to be creative and to apply their detailed knowledge to the redesign of business processes.

BPR Applicability in Manufacturing Industry

The following sub-sections describe current trends in the manufacturing industry and BPR applicability with respect to each of them. BPR has helped companies adapt to these trends enabling reduction in operating expenses, increase in profitability and get/sustain competitive advantage.

Processes are more important than the computer systems that support them. As such, processes should be fixed before installing any software to automate them. Once these processes straightened out, new systems can take companies to a completely new level. The following trends have facilitated and accelerated Manufacturing Process Improvements (MPI) significantly today. As such, most market leaders have embraced them and the rest are in process of embracing these through BPR.

Agile Manufacturing

Agile manufacturing enables businesses to be flexible on various facets. It includes 'leanness' because a high stock or spare capacity method of'providing flexibility to changing customer demands or adversity is not a viable financial option, but in addition it demands increased flexibility in terms of the ability to:

- Determine customer needs quickly, and continuously reposition the company against its competitors
- Design things quickly based on those individual needs
- Put them into full scale, quality, and production rapidly
- Respond to changing volumes and mix without delay
- Respond to a crisis quickly

> Being lean means—having the ability to quickly respond to customer demands. It also means—working with limited inventory, waste elimination and reacting on-the-fly, to changing conditions.

Agility is achieved through regular business process re-engineering, and re-segmenting of business processes including the manufacturing processes into 'virtual' transient organizations or teams, having individual or small customer group aligned objectives. It has major implications for:

- Organization
- Business processes
- Production processes and equipment
- People skill interchangeability
- Recruitment and training

Lean Manufacturing

Lean manufacturing is originally based on production systems used by Toyota. Being lean means—having the ability to quickly respond to customer demands. It also means—working with limited inventory, waste elimination and reacting on-the-fly, to changing conditions. The emphasis lies in the reduction of throughput times. The result is—a significant reduction in operating expenses, and increased customer satisfaction and retention.

Most Japanese companies were early embracers of lean manufacturing, but global manufacturing leaders today are implementing it through BPR.

Manufacturers that have embraced the concepts of lean manufacturing have found that significant gains can be achieved from putting process issues first and technology second.

Just-in-Time (JIT)

Just-in-Time (JIT) is a way of producing products on order, not before anybody has ordered the product. It also means that the product should be delivered 'in time'. Just-in-Time originally encapsulated the logistics aspects of the Toyota Production System.

A brief summary of JIT core principles is given below—these encapsulate key focus areas for BPR:

> Just-in-Time (JIT) is a way of producing products on order, not before anybody has ordered the product. It also means that the product should be delivered 'in time'.

- The use of ***multiple small machines*** (rather than "efficient" expensive machines that have to be kept busy).
- ***Group technology*** (commonly called 'Cellular' manufacturing)—it is based on the principle that product focused manufacturing is much simpler, with reduced material flows, as compared to factories where similar processes are grouped together, such as heat treatment.
- ***Production smoothing*** (levelled schedules) is based on the principle—smailis beautiful as far as batch sizes are

concerned, and that what is required is made when required without inflating batch sizes.

- ***Labour balancing*** highlights line imbalance from the cycle time of one operation to the next, and indicates the need to balance the manning for each operation (and the opportunity to improve the slowest to achieve balance).
- ***Set-up reduction***—the key factor in being able to reduce batch sizes, bottleneck first and perhaps stop there.
- ***Standard working*** (defined by the operator not the industrial engineer)—is a prescribed sequence of production steps performed by one operator, and balanced to the required rate of demand. It becomes the basis of understanding the job and therefore identifying what can be improved.
- ***Visual controls***—characteristic of JIT factories are simple visible controls, held locally where they are used to monitor key performance indicators, and used as a spur to improvement. This is a deliberate attempt to give eyeball control rather than the over-sophistication provided by remote computer systems
- ***Minimizing Inventory, Minimizing Work in Process and Synchronizing Production***

A just-in-time (JIT) or pull system implementation without any technology to add discipline to the process will fail badly. This is being used by most Japanese Auto Manufacturers. Auto OEMs are moving towards JIT in varying degrees, through BPR of their production and engineering divisions.

Collaborative Manufacturing

Collaborative manufacturing is also referred to as e-manufacturing. This is about re-thinking traditional processes and relationships with suppliers and customers, and enhancing them with technology in order to collaborate with trading partners in real time.

Sharing accurate real-time data is at the heart of e-manufacturing, which is the essence of business-to-business e-commerce.

> Collaborative manufacturing is also referred to as e-manuiacturing. This is about re-thinking traditional processes and relationships with suppliers and customers, and enhancing them with technology in order to collaborate with trading partners in real time.

Manufacturing partners must be willing to agree on a set of business practices to share information, and to compete as if they are one vertically-integrated company. This is enabled by technologies like internet, which help share information. While supply chain visibility and event management focus on order fulfillment activities, e-manufacturing looks at all of the processes involved in getting a product to market.

Key processes that can benefit from collaborative manufacturing currently are listed below and could be considered as candidates for BPR (to varying degrees depending on relative process maturity and strategic goals of manufacturers):

- *Planning and Scheduling*—includes forecasting and positioning of material for demand fulfillment and capacity management.
- *Product Design*—includes mechanical design, electrical design, test design and design for supply chains.
- *New Product Introduction*—includes bill of materials management, prototyping, design validation testing, and production validation testing.
- *Product Content Management*—includes change generation, change impact assessment, product change release, and change cut-in/phase in.

- *Order Management*—covers all activities from order capture to order tracking and exception management.
- *Sourcing*—includes approved vendor management, strategic sourcing and supplier selection.

Prime emphasis of collaborative manufacturing is to react to demand in real time. This entails that infrastructure issues need to be fixed first and other internal, core business processes like inventory control, etc need to be stream-lined in advance.

Intelligent Manufacturing

The goal of intelligent manufacturing is — "satisfying customer needs at the most efficient level for the lowest possible cost" by leveraging on automatic decision making capabilities built into manufacturing systems.

Intelligent manufacturing can be achieved in three basic ways:

- Existing manufacturing processes can become intelligent by monitoring and controlling the state of the manufacturing machine.
- Existing processes can be made intelligent by adding sensors to monitor and control the state of the product being processed.
- New processes can be intelligently designed to produce parts of the desired quality, without any need for sensing and controlling the process.

An intelligent manufacturing process has the ability to self-regulate and/or self-control to manufacture the product within the design specifications.

These concepts have been used in shop floor automation, assembly line automation, etc. In order to adapt to this concept, the focus is not only on automating systems, but re-designing dependent business processes around this leveraging on BPR.

For instance, software analysis and integration tools—collectively dubbed manufacturing intelligence systems—provide high-level views of factory-floor processes. These are used in typical manufacturing factories, sprawled over several acres, with thousands of production assets managed by several different control systems that need to be maintained in order to avoid faults in the process that could hamper production. They act *as* data collection tools, help in preventive maintenance, ensuring high production equipment uptimes.

> The goal of intelligent manufacturing is—"satisfying customer needs at the most efficient level for the lowest possible cost" by leveraging on automatic decision-making capabilities built into manufacturing systems.

Production Planning

Most large manufacturing companies (Hi-tech, Auto, etc) have used business process reengineering to improve inefficient, human-based and highly manual manufacturing lines, and to improve management's ability to make informed decisions around production issues.

Historically, manufacturers ran a 'push process' in which separate products were built on a shared production line, by running large batches and then re-setting the entire line for the next product. This 'make to stock' process required labour-intensive equipment and materials re-set, offering little ability to adapt production to market demand or to meet corporate financial deadlines.

During the business process re-engineering effort, manufacturers recognized that technology could be used as the key enabler to drive business logic and automated workflow into their production line. In fact, technologies like BPM (Business Process Management) include tools to analyze, define, model, automate, execute. monitor, change and administer business processes.

This business process re-engineering effort leveraging on appropriate technologies allows the manufacturer to move to a "pull" or "build to order" production method. The process begins when the customer places an order and a part is placed on the manufacturing line. In the pull process, the line can accommodate multiple products at one time and parts are automatically routed to their appropriate locations. Using sensors to recognize items on the line and complex business rules to 'direct the traffic'; this method successfully automates routing to differentiated station stops based on the product being built.

In the past, decision-making around production changes was difficult and time-consuming. Management had to read production schedules iine-by-line and could only make changes on a weekly basis. Today, through process re-design and technology leverage, the manufacturer is able to obtain a holistic look at production and alter the schedule on a daily basis in an effort to recognize revenue faster, thus pleasing its customers and investors. For example, the manufacturer can look up specific customers in the system and prioritize large orders for immediate production. Management now has more agility and can make decisions quickly in response to shifts in market conditions.

Key Business Benefits from this effort include:

- ***Flexible, multi-purpose production line,*** allowing greater responsiveness to market demand through a 'make to order' process, which reduced space requirements
- ***Increased productivity***
- Providing *management* with greater *visibility into production schedule,* giving the *ability to adjust production plans to meet market demands* and achieve corporate financial goals

- *Increase in Revenue* through *jCost Reduction,* facilitated through *increased Agility of Production Lines*

Product Design and Development

New product development has been recognized as one of the key growth drivers today, propelling manufacturers to future success. In addition, focusing R&D expenditures on shorter-term specific business opportunities has been recognized, as a very effective corporate strategy for manufacturing companies to attain their competitive advantage.

These factors bring special emphasis on streamlining business processes, systems and operations around product design, development and data management. Traditionally this has been maintained through a plethora of in-house proprietary, inflexible and redundant systems. Most large and mid-size manufacturers have ventured into business process re-engineering efforts in this space to primarily reduce their operating expenses, increase profits, and sustain their competitive advantage. Wipro has helped a large global auto (OEM) manufacturer leverage on PLM solutions to streamline product design and development processes in its product engineering divisions.

A brief summary of core BPR focus areas is given below:

- ***Collaborative, Concurrent Engineering and Design Processes*:** Streamline and shorten the complex and time-consuming process of design and manufacturing as this enables all the participants in the process—designer, manufacturer, supplier and consumer—to share the same engineering database and fulfill their roles at the same time. This shortens the design-production cycle, significantly reducing the cost of changes that occur in the design of parts during the manufacturing change. Overall, divisional competitiveness is improved through this seamless interaction.

- *Integrated Product and Process Development* through teamwork and task optimization.
- *Share and Control Product Data during planning,* design, production and maintenance cycles.
- *Cost Control and Operational Improvement:* Increase in profits achieved through:
  - ❖ Shortened product development cycles
  - ❖ Increase introduction success rates—go to market sooner than competition
  - ❖ Streamlining business processes around product design, development and data management
  - ❖ Re-using parts, drawings, data and documents
  - ❖ Improving product safety and quality
  - ❖ Production efficiency facilitated through adoption of best practices
  - ❖ Meet government requirements
  - ❖ Change in Attitude—*"Do it better—do it faster"*
  - ❖ Involving Customer—enable customers to view product development through various stages and seek their inputs/approval
  - ❖ Streamlining communication internally and between business partners and suppliers

> New product development has been recognized as one ol the key growth drivers today, propelling manufacturers to future success. In addition, focussing R&D expenditures on shorter-term specific business opportunities has been recognized as a very effective corporate strategy, for manufacturing companięs to attain their competitive advantage.

Supply Chain Management

As more and more companies open up shop on the Web, traditional ways of doing business are becoming extinct. This is especially true in the manufacturing sector, where the internet is reducing costs, decreasing processing time, and opening up new opportunities for small and medium-sized companies. In the past, only large, multinational manufacturers could sell their products to a worldwide customer base. Now, web-enabled businesses of any size can buy, sell, or barter goods around the globe and ensure that their partners and customers remain satisfied.

The internet is also transforming the conventional supply chain. Formerly, a product had to travel a long road from the design table to the customer's doorstep, passing from manufacturer to supplier to retailer, and even one or more resellers, before reaching its final destination. By using the web to process orders, manufacturers are eliminating much of the cost and bureaucracy from the supply chain, speeding up inventory turn-around, and decreasing response time to market trends, in addition, a web-enabled supply chain allows business leaders to view and understand their customers' purchasing habits and preferences.

The dilemma for manufacturers is not whether they should extend their enterprises to the web, but how Supply chain management systems enable end-to-end management and tracking flow of material, information and revenue, from the manufacturing floor to customers. Investing in the wrong solution could be tremendously costly, and more importantly, could squander valuable time in a marketplace where the speed of business is accelerating.

In addition, ERPs have existed for a while now, but not all companies who've invested on it reaped all the benefits of ERP. The business processes around procurement in an enterprise need to be optimized first and then leverage on technology as a key enabler.

To succeed in the new marketplace, manufacturers must be able to compete with other web-enabled firms to keep costs low, maintain high customer satisfaction rates, and ensure a visible corporate profile. In order to facilitate this, there's a huge emphasis on building lean supply chains.

Key BPR focus areas for building lean supply chains include:

- *Networked Supply-Chain Management:* A networked supply-chain management system links every member in the supply chain—from partners and suppliers to manufacturers and retailers. It integrates a company's internal systems, including those for inventory, payment processing, marketing, accounts, and order tracking. It expedites order fulfillment by directly linking suppliers and customers It maximizes inventory visibility and ensures that a company has products in stock when customers are ready to buy.
- *E-Marketplaces (Web-based Trading Communities):* This offers manufacturers, a cost-effective and comprehensive means to extend their enterprises. E-Marketplaces function as industry-specific procurement centers for manufacturers and their customers. They offer a broad sales channel for products and bring together new buyers and sellers via the internet, giving manufacturers access to trading partners worldwide.
- *Agile Demand Management:* It is the ability to provide forecasts throughout the supply chain of forthcoming encountered demand, in current without the supply chains. buffering It is a significant challenge to the transparency of demand through the supply chain, without the intervention of inventory planners. For example, the ethic of production planning is to create a stable plan for manufacturing to produce efficiently.

Agility requires constant change of plans and very short lead-times. There is a switch of emphasis here — from factory stability, to rhe customer need. This has a major impact on production planning and control, in that in essence a product is earmarked for a particular customer fairly early on in the process so that customization may proceed from that point.

By using the web to process orders, manufacturers are eliminating much of the cost and bureaucracy from the supply chain, speeding up inventory turn-around, and decreasing response time to market trends. In addition, a web-enabled supply chain allows business leaders to view and understand their customers' purchasing habits and preferences.

A combination of these three—networked supply chains, e-marketplaces and agile demand management—are powerful and crucial to lean supply chain design. When judiciously combined, they dramatically improve a manufacturer's operations and its bottom line by:

- Increasing profitability and efficiency by replacing manual contract bidding, procurement, and payment processes, with secure networked transactions
- Improving planning and forecasting through real-time sharing of design and research data
- Enhancing supply-chain management through inventory flexibility and international order outsourcing
- Raising a company's visibility and help it to acquire new customers

Wipro has contributed significantly to the eSCM initiative of a large, global airframe manufacturer in designing and implementing SCM solutions, leveraging on BPM technologies to automate the entire parts supply contract management life cycle. This has resulted in shortened and more efficient process cycles at every stage in contract processing, increased visibility through dashboard metrics at the enterprise level, increased employee productivity and tangible improvements to bottom line.

> BPR lays special emphasis on optimizing business processes first and leverage on technology as a key enabler in this initiative, ii appropriate. Both process streamlining and technology leverage to the right extent compliment each other and are equally important.

Conclusion

Manufacturers the world over, have/are applying organizational structural changes and adopting corporate strategies that are radical in nature to steer through an increasingly tough and slow growth global economy Organizational structural changes include core focus on core business, flattened corporate structure, merged with/acquired new companies, de-centralized business units, global business units and centralization of core administrative activities. Key corporate strategies rated very effective include global branding, reduced operating expenses, focused R&D on shorter-term specific business opportunities, more strategic alliances with customers, suppliers and competitors and value chain management strategies. The emphasis is on driving profit/loss responsibility deeper into the organization.

Manufacturers are re-aligning their organizations with these corporate strategies through business process re-engineering. BPR facilitates organization re-design. BPR helps organizations in re-thinking on each of the competitive priorities — quality, price, delivery speed, delivery reliability, flexibility and innovation. It facilitates organizations in adopting to latest trends in the manufacturing industry, all of which lay prime emphasis on maximizing performance, reduction in operating expenses, bottom-line improvement, increased customer satisfaction and retention, and constantly sustain competitive advantage. It helps organizations to concentrate on maintaining performance in 'qualifying' factors and improving 'competitive edge' factors.

As a concluding thought, it's worth highlighting the fact that BPR lays special emphasis on optimizing business processes first and leverage on technology as a key enabler in this initiative, if appropriate. Both process streamlining and technology leverage to the right extent compliment each other and are equally important The two go 'hand in glove' to facilitate radically re-designed business processes resulting in significant productivity and performance gains.

In essence, BPR is more relevant to the manufacturing industry today, than ever before.

REFERENCES

Business Process Re-engineering—Beakpoint Strategies for Market Dominance, Johansson and Henry

Business Process Re-engineering—Johansson, McHugh, Pendleburg & Wheeler III

McHugh, Merli & Wheeler—Beyond Business Process Re-engineering—Towards the Holonic Enterprise, Publisher: John Wiley & Sons

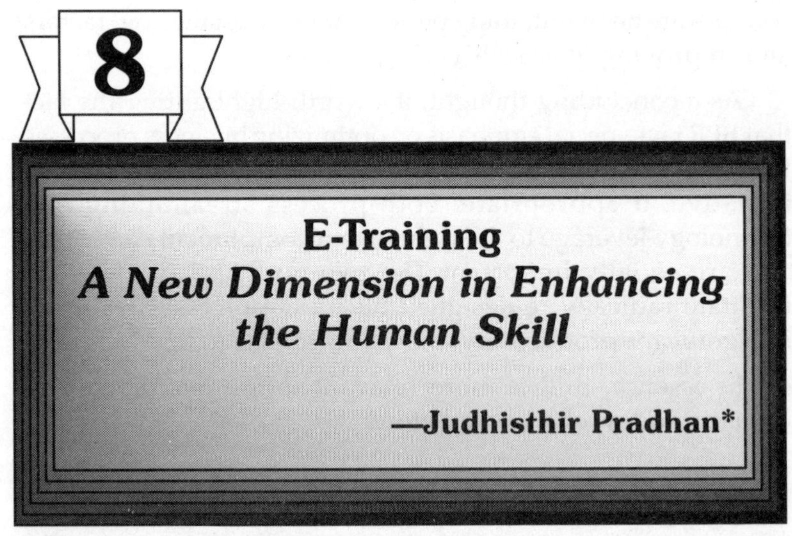

8

E-Training
A New Dimension in Enhancing the Human Skill

—Judhisthir Pradhan*

Introduction and Meaning

Training is one of the most vital part of HR department of any sector. The skilled hands not only increase the productivity and quality but also save for the organization which is very important and vital. The new and modern technologies now changed the scenario of all tradition pattern and now it is the time to train the employees on mouse click. Yes, I am talking about E-Training. E-Training may be defined as" *The delivery of a learning, training or education programme by electronic means. E-learning involves the use of a computer or electronic device (e.g. a mobile phone) in some way to provide training, educational or learning material.* (Derek Stockley 2003)". E-learning can involve a greater variety of equipment than online training or education, for as the name implies, 'online' involves using the Internet

* Faculty Member, Dept. of MBA, S.M. University, Berhampur Centre, Orissa.

or an Intranet. CD-ROM and DVD can be used to provide learning materials. Distance education provided the base for e-learning's development. E-learning can be 'on demand'. It overcomes timing, attendance and travel difficulties. Online training courses allow one to learn at convenient time and places. It is not only beneficial to the employee but also beneficial to the organization and the trainer. Electronic media has been in use for many years. Lots of persons who have adopted these technologies are saying that they have got tremendous results and in the same time many scholars have criticized the techniques from various grounds. This paper is an attempt pros and cons of E-training.

Scope and Objective of the Study

As the present time is getting so precious and busy, it is not at all possible to have grip on every segment of the work force directly. Every organization now wants to be an MNC. The motive of wealth and profit maximization is encouraging the investor of the entrepreneurs to have more workforce as well as utmost of reach, but in this competitive world training directly to all segment of workforce seems difficult. Hence many organizations have started training the employees through internet and web sites. In India though this concept is not so popular and vastly adopted but keeping the future issues in mind it is necessary to think in this direction.

CSCW, CSCL and CSCT

In 1980's CSCW was introduced to define systems that can support network working. It is defined as a computer-based network system that supports group work in a common task and provides a shared interface for groups to work with. The CSCW (Computer supported Collaborative Work) tends to focus on communication technology themselves that are used mainly in the business setting. These communication technologies can be used to assist organizations in various ways:

- Reserving and retrieving knowledge management data that is embedded in the everyday work to improve the quality of the offered services and the workers satisfaction.

- Encouraging worker to communicate, co-operate, co-ordinate, solve problems, compete, and negotiate to establish human relationships in working settings.
- Supporting groups that are small project-oriented teams that have important tasks and strict deadlines.
- Supporting the processes that lead to management decisions.

The need for flexible and supportive communication structures at different discipline has caused the CSCW to grow out into a wider number of researchers, particularly the Computer Supported Collaborative Learning (CSCL). In the last decade, the development of CSCL domain has been remarkable . CSCL systems have highlighted the importance of social interactions in the E Learning environment . CSCL is an interdisciplinary domain (software engineering and education) whose main objective is to allow instructors to become directly involved in designing collaborative activities in the online environment . The interest of applying CSCL in training programmes is increasingly noticed. As a result, a new discipline CSCT, Computer Supported Collaborative Training, is currently emerging, which its primary goal is to promote active learning style into training programmes. The process of knowledge construction can be effectively achieved in training programs by engaging the trainees in activities that involve internal negotiation and deliberate actions, such as goal setting, negotiation, identification, and discussion of problems and their solutions.

CSCT Tools

CSCT tools can be divided in two categories: asynchronous tools and synchronous tools.

Asynchronous tools enable communication and collaboration at 'anytime, anyplace', providing more management freedom. These types of tools are appropriate for collaborations that require more time for reflection. Synchronous tools enable 'same-time, anyplace' collaboration, providing immediacy and faster response, which enhances spontaneous thinking skills.

Many systems have been developed to support collaborative learning in the online environment, using some of the most common tools in CSCT. We start by listing some of the tools found in the asynchronous collaboration environment and how they can be used for training sessions:

- ***Forums***: This is the most used tool within the asynchronous environment. It can be used to facilitate topical discussions through which trainers can use it to create threads of topics to be discussed by trainees.
- *Q&A:* This tool can be used by trainees to post their questions regarding various training issues. Other trainees who have the same questions can reuse these answers.
- ***E-mail***: It is usually used by trainers and trainees to send and receive notifications and communications.
- ***Wiki***: Trainees can use wiki to create a set of documents that reflect shared knowledge within training group. Wikis can be used to facilitate knowledge-broadcasting and idea exchanging.
- ***Weblogs***: The weblogs or blogs can be introduced as a place in which trainees are encouraged to initiate training topics discussion, comments, notes, etc. in order to create and share personal knowledge. The main tools found in the synchronous collaboration environment are listed below:
- ***Text chat***: This is a text-based communication tool that trainers and trainees can use to instantly elaborate, brainstorm, argue, and discuss during the training session. There might be various chatting settings to

accommodate various interaction types, such as private, public, restricted, etc.

- ***Audio/video conferencing tools***: These enable trainers to present their lectures in the online environment. They can be also used to facilitate groups' virtual meetings and role playing.
- ***Polling tools***: They enable trainees to vote on certain topics or issues.
- ***Application-sharing tools:*** Application-sharing tools allow instructors trainers in demonstrating to remote trainees how to use certain software applications.
- ***Whiteboard tools:*** A whiteboard simulates the communication that occurs when instructors draw on the class blackboard.
- ***File-sharing tools***: They allow participants to upload their resources to share them with each others. Various technical limitations have caused asynchronous tools to be used more in recent years. Nevertheless, synchronous tools are starting to move forward, due to recent advances in both bandwidth and mobile technology. The advances and widespread adoption of mobile systems provide users with more flexibility to access synchronous sessions. Nevertheless, designing synchronous collaborative activity is considered to be more resource intensive (facilitator's time, effective planning, appropriate technical background, etc.) than the traditional way of training . General synchronous tools (chat, whiteboard, etc.) that are proposed to support informal synchronous training are not always appropriate or sufficient to build a meaningful learning experience. In the past few years, a large number of applications have focused on providing computer support for collaboration. Most of these applications started at universities and/or other research institutions. Their aim has been to solve the primary

needs of supporting collaborative learning across different organisations and platforms. In this section we introduce some of these applications that could be used for CSCT:

- ***Breeze***: This is a commercial software, originally produced by Macromedia and now by Adobe, as a rich web communication system that provides online meeting, collaboration, real-time web conferencing, and live presentations. Breeze enables instructors to easily create engaging communications that include voice, video, and animations. Breeze has four main components:

  Breeze Meeting: It supports large-scale meetings and small collaborative group meetings. It provides audio/video communication, application-sharing, and white boarding.

  Breeze Training: It provides online training. Trainers can use this product to deploy, track, and manage online courses. Computer Support for Activity-based E- Training

  Breeze Presenter: It allows designing of media-rich content by including voice annotation and insertion of polls and quizzes into PowerPoint slides.

  Breeze Event: It manages trainees' registration, qualifications, notification, automatic e-mail reminders, and tracking.

- *LAMS* : This is open-source software, developed by Macquarie University. The intention of LAMS is to enable instructors to design a sequence of learning activities for trainees that includes content and collaborative tasks. LAMS provides trainers with a set of collaborative tools that can be easily dragged and dropped to design sequences of collaborative tasks. It allows instructors to runs the sequence of tasks for trainees and allows them to monitor and track trainee progress.

- *RELOAD*: This is an open-source authoring environment, developed at the University of Bolton. Its main aim is to allow instructors to author learning designs based on activities. A single activity could be any form of learning activity, such as reading a learning material, collaborating with peers, visiting a museum, etc. The RELOAD Editor allows trainers to design a unit of training session by sequencing learning activities in a simple format. In each step, instructors need to specify at least the task description. They can also include reading resources or communication service in each step. The RELOAD Player is used to run the design.
- *Beehive*: This is a high-level specialised learning design authoring tool for collaborative learning, developed at the University of Sydney. Beehive tool enables instructors to easily create potentially effective collaborative training designs by particularising and customising some of the best practices in collaborative learning, according to the requirements and conditions of a particular training scenario.

CSCT and Collaborative Learning Patterns

Designing successful training programmes is a challenging task. Instructional design is a systematic approach to course development which ensures that specific learning objectives are accomplished. It focuses on structuring learning process in an appropriate way within certain pedagogy that makes training more efficient. The pattern approach currently draws more attention for identifying collaborative patterns within traditional training programme settings. Some of collaborative patterns are currently used in the face-to-face training settings, such as Brainstorming, Role-Playing, Group Discussion, Debriefing, Case Study, Debate, Pro Contra. There has developed a new awareness of the role of these collaborative patterns in training systems development. For example, in the authors describe how two CLP, jigsaw and pyramid, are transformed into software development design patterns. This study also involved integrating the two design patterns. Nevertheless, the pattern of interaction in collaborative training changes dynamically with the requirements and constraints of the situation. The process involves the interaction of multiple goals of different scope and nature. As a result, a single training session:

- Could contain more than one consecutive collaborative patterns or in parallel.
- Should support instructors/trainers in applying and adapting a training model to the situation at hand.
- Should even support instructors/trainers in modifying the underlying model and creating new training models out of these collaborative learning patterns.

CSCT Cases

Many successful workshop/training processes, such as customer relationship management, business goal setting, and improvement planning, are usually delivered using classroom presentations, followed.

1. Retailing Session's Scenario

The session's face-to-face scenario was as follows:

1. Download and read individually the documentation regarding the product education.
2. Each participant privately writes down his considerations about customer's questions: What is being proposed, what's in it for them? Why they need the products and why should they believe in our product? How quick and reliable are deliveries and what is the money back guarantee? Are they value for money?

3. Each participant brainstorms within his group on ways of securing, servicing and retaining customers.
4. Participants brainstorm with the entire class's participants all the benefits of the products.
5. Each participant discusses within his group as many questions about the product.
6. Each participant role-play retailer and associate to practice answering questions explaining benefits, delivering basic facts and a personal story.
7. A final debriefing session to conclude all findings and recommendations. This scenario employs multiple collaborative patterns (Brainstorm, Role-playing, and Group Discussion), which were used to support instructors in applying the retailing training model. Furthermore, this session scenario could be applied to other training models, such as Prospecting, and Goal setting.

2. Sport Case

Online training in sport imposes additional challenges, since it is traditionally performed in physical places (courts, for example). This particular sport-oriented face-to-face session was conducted within netball team. The session was designed to teach a particular skill, that is, "how to make one breaking zone from back-line throwing". The computer supported session was designed to be conducted after performing a physical training activity on the court and explaining to trainees the desired skill. The session's objective was to identify things that did not go well, after viewing several videos. The session structure followed the Problem-based Learning Technique (but with some customisation) as follows:

1. Trainees are asked to watch a video section.
2. Trainees need to identify what went wrong.
3. Trainees are asked to brainstorm some solutions.

4. Trainees are asked to discuss these solutions within their group.
5. Trainees are asked to draw on a still image how to apply these solutions.
6. The chairperson is asked to report on his group's considerations

E-Training at Corporate Level

Leading corporates across the globe are now adopting e-Training in order to make the training more flexible, impactive, time saving, cost-effective and efficient. Few examples are:

Axa, The French Solution

The growth of e-learning training in France has been slow, when compared to the United States. While e-learning makes for 60 per cent of the expenses of corporate training in the U.S., in France it makes for only 11 per cent. Surveys of French companies indicate that face to face is still the preferred training model and that many human resources employees are not clear about the e-learning potential as a training tool. Axa is among the exceptions. Axa is a multinational insurance group with close to 100,000 employees in 25 countries. Like many other large companies, Axa was having difficulties in providing training to its large and scattered workforce. However, sending employees out for training or bringing trainers to its different branches was becoming increasingly complex and expensive. Axa's Human Resources Department, in France, decided to use their Intranet connection to develop a distance learning programme based on modules, which would ensure a fast distribution for a large audience. The modular structure made it easier and less costly to establish a schedule of frequent reviews of the content material to maintain the curriculum updated. The company started its e-learning training project in 1997. It entered into partnership with IBM for the technical aspects of the training and with other partners for the production of educational material. Before starting the project, the Human Resources Department organized a five-day retreat with the managers where they had to play a game of opening new markets using only telephone and portable computers to communicate. The exercise gave the managers an opportunity to rethink their views about ICTs and their potential. After ensuring the managers' support, the Department met with the employees to discuss the changes and teach them how to use the Intranet for training purposes. Only then, the Department began to gradually introduce e-learning strategies in the employees' traditional training schedule. The pilot stage provided good results and some important lessons, including the following:

Supervisors' support is essential for the success of any training project; they must be allies, rather than barriers to employees' training.

- It is important to have a place reserved for the training process and someone to encourage and prod the trainee; few individuals will have the self-discipline to search for training independently.
- Developing training materials for multinational workforces is a major challenge, since learning preferences vary across countries—for instance, the Anglo-Saxons preferred to begin with anecdotes and move into the general, while the French preferred to look at the general and move into the particular, and the Germans required traditional structures. Training varies between 40 and 400 hours per employee.

The employee can go through the training individually or with a tutor's help. Tutors are experts in the content area who volunteer to work with the distance education experts. They can be reached by mail, telephone or face-to-face. Piloted in one of the French branches, e-learning training is now available to all Axa employees worldwide.

Carrefour, A Brazilian Experience

Carrefour is probably the largest wholesale chain in Brazil, with almost 50,000 employees. The chain, founded in 1963 in France, has a long tradition of employee training. In the late 1980s, Carrefour had founded one of the first 'corporate universities' in the world, the Institute Marcel Founder, and was using video-conferencing for employee training. Currently, the chain has three 'corporate universities,' one of them in Sao Paulo, Brazil—the Institute de Formafao Carrefour (Carrefour Training Institute). The universities offer a variety of training not only to employees, but also to clients and vendors. The Brazilian Institute provides 114 courses in different areas that include informatics, marketing, management, etc. The programmes have different platforms, including multimedia, video, DVD, television broadcast via satellite, and Intranet. The training programmes vary from four hours to 15 days. Some courses are mandatory while others are elective and participation depends on the interests of the employee and his or her supervisor. Courses can also be provided on site, and the Institute has many training rooms in addition to a large auditorium with simultaneous translation capabilities. At this time, the Institute is serving only employees, but training programmes for clients and vendors are programmed to open late this year. Plans for expansion also include courseon the Internet and a mix of online and face-to-face strategies. In less than one year of functioning, the Institute has trained about 3,000 employees.

The reasons Carrefour moved into e-learning are similar to Axa's. As the chain spread throughout the country, the distance between stores and training centers pushed costs up; e-learning provides economies with traveling costs and reduces the time that employees are away from work. E-learning also avoids the complex logistics of planning and implementing training for large numbers of individuals coming from many different places. In addition, it is easier and less expensive to actualize e-learning material than printed material. The company also perceived a need to maintain a technological lead. According to the Institute's Training Director, "The majority of large businesses in the world is investing in online training . .. and some are well advanced in this area. We could not be left behind."

Cisco Learning Network

Cisco Systems is one of the largest network companies in the world with annual revenues of over US$20 billion. Headquartered in the U.S.A., the company has 225 sales and support offices in 75 countries. For years, its training programmes were managed independently at each different unit, resulting in redundant and unequal programming. To streamline, expedite and improve the quality of the training programmes, the Company developed the Cisco Learning Network (CLN). CLN training contents are developed using multimedia technologies and stored in a centralized database. The employee selects either a full curriculum or individual modules and takes an assessment test. The test results guide the adaptation of the module to respond to the employee's individual needs. The employee is evaluated at different intervals to gauge the effectiveness of the programme, and results are stored in a personal training file in the human resources database. E-learning programmes can be provided in two ways: (1) in scheduled delivery, at fixed time and place or (2) on-demand, for individuals who have particular needs. Scheduled delivery uses three platforms: multicasts (videos that are sent over the network to desktops), virtual classrooms, and remote laboratories. On-demand training uses web-based on demand content, CD-ROM, and remote labs. The laboratories are used to supplement complex topics. They include simulations that provide virtual access to equipment and techniques too costly to be available for every learner. The CLN system promotes significant savings of time away from work—it was observed that CLN courses reduced the time that the sales employees spent away from their customers by up to 40 per cent. Cisco's training expertise has outgrown the corporation and the company is now a major developer of training solutions. The Cisco Networking Academy Programme prepares high school and college students in how to design, build and maintain computer networks. There are more than 6,000 academies spread through all 50 American states. The Academies reflect partnerships between the company and private or governmental organizations, including public schools. Other training activities provided by Cisco include online seminars and Career Certifications programmes. The certification programme has grown from 6,000 students per year to 100,000 and is offered online or through more than 130 sites and 750 certified instructors worldwide. Some of the courses are offered by Cisco Learning Partners—organizations authorized to deliver Cisco-developed learning content.

Advantages of E-Learning

Followings are some advantages of E-Learning:

- Saving of a lot of time which usually one spends during the traveling for training.
- As CDS, DVDs, web pages are available a trainee can use the training tips at any moment of time.
- It cost effective both for the training provider and the trainee.
- As it is not a so called class room training, hence the trainee may take training as per his comfort ness which add an extra value to the learning.
- As there is no time bar, hence the trainee may access the training at any moment.
- It allows the trainee to discuss with the trainer in details and can clarify his doubts which he may not ask in classroom training due to lack of time or unfavourable circumstances.

- It doesn't create burden on the employee but increases his efficiency.
- It doesn't pressurize the employee.

Disadvantages of E-Learning

Fallowings are some disadvantages of e-learning.

- In the absence of the trainer physically the training may not be taken seriously by the trainee.
- The trainee may neglect or take may take more time to understand the training tips.
- The trainee must be a computer literate
- The trainee should have convenience resources for accessing the tools and aids provide to him.

Conclusion

Although e-training has some positive impact and negative impact, but the present scenario says that it is the time's demand. Hence we must adopt it but in such a manner in which it will be fruitful. Many organizations and corporations have adopted this and has got good result too. But in Indian context a lot has to be done. Most of our employees are not that much of able to understand the e-training, but a continuous process and approach may stand us in the world class. Adopting the latest technology is always welcomable but proper utilization of the technology is most essential.

REFERENCES

International Journal of Learning Technology, Vol. 1

Campus-wide Information Systems, Vol. 23

G. Palmer, R. Peters, and R. Streetman. (2003). "Cooperative Learning." Emerging Perspectives on Learning, Teaching, and Technology Retrieved 22 Augest 2006

Dimitracopoulou and A. Petrou, "Advanced Collaborative Distance Learning Systems for Young Students: Design Issues and Current Trends on New Cognitive and Metacognitive Tools"

Education International Journal, Vol. 4

J. B. Willfams and J. Jacobs, "Exploring the use of Blogs as Learning Spaces in the Higher Education Sector," Australasian Journal of Educational Technology, Vol. 20

Adobe. Retrieved 22 May 2006, from http://www.adobe.com/products/breeze/index.html.

LAMS. "The Learning Activity Management System." Retrieved 12 March 2006, from http://www.lamsinternational.com.

N. Shambaugh and S. Magliaro, "A Reflexive Model for Teaching Instructional Design"

Educational Technology Research and Development, Vol. 49

www.TechKnowLogia.org

http://www.zdnet.fr/actu/busi/a0018468.html.

http://www.zdnet.fr/actu/busi/a0018470.html.

Business Process Reengineering (BPR) is a management practice that aims to improve the efficiency of the business process. The key to BPR is for organizations to look at their business processes from a 'clean slate' perspective and determine how they can best construct these processes to improve how they conduct business. Re-engineering is a fundamental rethinking and radical redesign of business processes to achieve dramatic improvements in cost, quality, speed, and service. BPR combines a strategy of promoting business innovation with a strategy of making major improvements to business processes so that a company can become a much stronger and more successful competitor in the marketplace.

Re-engineering is the basis for many recent developments in management. The cross-functional team, for example, has become popular because of the desire to re-engineer separate

* Selection Grade Lecturer in Commerce Govt. Degree Narsannapeta Srikakulam District Andhra University, A.P.

functional tasks into complete cross-functional processes. Also, many recent management information systems developments aim to integrate a wide number of business functions. Enterprise resource planning, supply chain management, knowledge management systems, groupware and collaborative systems, Human Resource Management Systems and customer relationship management systems all owe a debt to re-engineering theory.

Business Process Re-engineering is also known as Business Process Redesign, Business Transformation, or Business Process Change Management.

Overview

Business process re-engineering (BPR) began as a private sector technique to help organizations fundamentally rethink how they do their work in order to dramatically improve customer service, cut operational costs, and become world-class competitors. A key stimulus for re-engineering has been the continuing development and deployment of sophisticated information systems and networks. Leading organizations are becoming bolder in using this technology to support innovative business processes, rather than refining current ways of doing work.

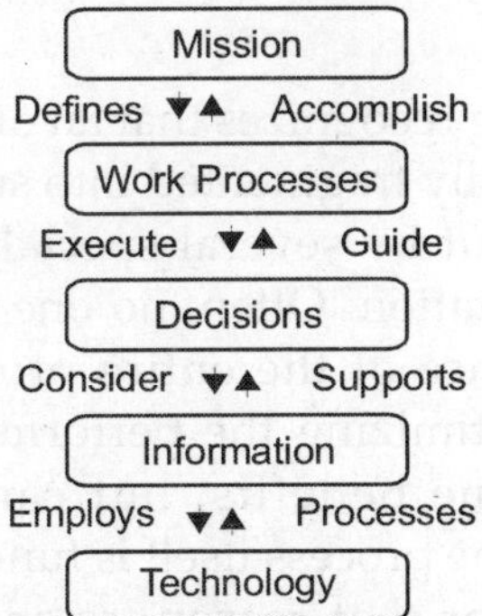

Re-engineering guidance and relationship of Mission and Work Processes to Information Technology.

Business process re-engineering is one approach for redesigning the way work is done to better support the organization's mission and reduce costs. Reengineering starts with a high-level assessment of the organization's mission, strategic goals, and customer needs. Basic questions are asked, such as "Does our mission need to be redefined? Are our strategic goals aligned with our mission? Who are our customers?" An organization may find that it is operating on questionable assumptions, particularly in terms of the wants and needs of its customers. Only after the organization rethinks what it should be doing, does it go on to decide how best to do it.

Within the framework of this basic assessment of mission and goals, reengineering focuses on the organization's business processes—the steps and procedures that govern how resources are used to create products and services that meet the needs of particular customers or markets. As a structured ordering of work steps across time and place, a business process can be decomposed into specific activities, measured, modelled, and improved. It can also be completely redesigned or eliminated altogether. Re-engineering identifies, analyzes, and redesigns an organization's core business processes with the aim of achieving dramatic improvements in critical performance measures, such as cost, quality, service, and speed.

Re-engineering recognizes that an organization's business processes are usually fragmented into subprocesses and tasks that are carried out by several specialized functional areas within the organization. Often, no one is responsible for the overall performance of the entire process. Re-engineering maintains that optimizing the performance of subprocesses can result in some benefits, but cannot yield dramatic improvements if the process itself is fundamentally inefficient and outmoded. For that reason, re-engineering focuses on redesigning the process as a whole in order to achieve the greatest possible benefits to the organization and their customers. This drive for realizing dramatic improvements by fundamentally rethinking how the organization's work should be done distinguishes re-engineering from process improvement efforts that focus on functional or incremental improvement.

History

In 1990, Michael Hammer, a former professor of computer science at the Massachusetts Institute of Technology (MIT), published an article in the *Harvard Business Review,* in which he claimed that the major challenge for managers is to obliterate non-value adding work, rather than using technology for automating it. This statement implicitly accused managers of having focused on the wrong issues, namely that technology in general, and more specifically information technology, has been used primarily for automating existing processes rather than using it as an enabler for making non-value adding work obsolete.

Hammer's claim was simple: Most of the work being done does not add any value for customers, and this work should be removed, not accelerated through automation. Instead, companies should reconsider their processes in order to maximize customer value, while minimizing the consumption of resources required for delivering their product or service. A similar idea was advocated by Thomas H. Davenport and J. Short in 1990, at that time a member of the Ernst & Young research center, in a paper published in the *Sloan Management Review* the same year as Hammer published his paper.

This idea, to unbiasedly review a company's business processes, was rapidly adopted by a huge number of firms, which were striving for renewed competitiveness, which they had lost due to the market entrance of foreign competitors, their inability to satisfy customer needs, and their insufficient cost structure. Even well established management thinkers, such as Peter Drucker and Tom Peters, were accepting and advocating BPR as a new tool for (re-)achieving success in a dynamic world. During the following years, a fast growing number of publications, books as well as journal articles, were dedicated to BPR, and many consulting firms embarked on this trend and developed BPR methods. However, the critics were fast to claim that BPR was a way to dehumanize the work place, increase managerial control, and to justify downsizing, i.e. major reductions of the work force, and a rebirth of Taylorism under a different label.

Despite this critique, reengineering was adopted at an accelerating pace and by 1993, as many as 65 per cent of the Fortune 500 companies claimed to either have initiated re-engineering efforts, or to have plans to do so. This trend was fueled by the fast adoption of BPR by the consulting industry, but also by the study *Made in America,* conducted by MIT, that showed how companies in many US industries had lagged behind their foreign counterparts in terms of competitiveness, time-to-market and productivity.

Development after 1995

With the publication of critiques in 1995 and 1996 by some of the early BPR proponents, coupled with abuses and misuses of the concept by others, the reengineering fervor in the U.S. began to wane. Since then, considering business processes as a starting point for business analysis and redesign has become a widely accepted approach and is a standard part of the change methodology portfolio, but is typically performed in a less radical way as originally proposed.

More recently, the concept of Business Process Management (BPM) has gained major attention in the corporate world and can be considered as a successor to the BPR wave of the 1990s, as it is evenly driven by a striving for process efficiency supported by information technology. Equivalently to the critique brought forward against BPR, BPM is now accused of focusing on technology and disregarding the people aspects of change.

Business Process Re-engineering Topics

Definition

Different definitions can be found. This section contains the definition provided in notable publications in the field:

- "...the fundamental rethinking and radical redesign of business processes to achieve dramatic improvements in critical contemporary measures of performance, such as cost, quality, service, and speed."
- "encompasses the envisioning of new work strategies, the actual process design activity, and the implementation of the change in all its complex technological, human, and organizational dimensions."

Additionally, Davenport (ibid.) points out the major difference between BPR and other approaches to organization development (OD), especially the continuous improvement or TQM movement, when he states: "Today firms must seek not fractional, but multiplicative levels of improvement—10x rather than 10 per cent." Finally, Johansson provide a description of BPR relative to other process-oriented views, such as Total Quality Management (TQM) and Just-in-time (JIT), and state:

> "Business Process Re-engineering, although a close relative, seeks radical rather than merely continuous improvement. It escalates the efforts of JIT and TQM to make process orientation a strategic tool and a core competence of the organization. BPR concentrates on core business processes, and uses the specific techniques within the JIT and TQM 'toolboxes' as enablers, while broadening the process vision."

In order to achieve the major improvements BPR is seeking for, the change of structural organizational variables, and other ways of managing and performing work is often considered as being insufficient. For being able to reap the achievable benefits fully, the use of information technology (IT) is conceived as a major contributing factor. While IT traditionally has been used for supporting the existing business functions, i.e. it was used for increasing organizational efficiency, it now plays a role as enabler of new organizational forms, and patterns of collaboration within and between organizations.

BPR derives its existence from different disciplines, and four major areas can be identified as being subjected to change in BPR—organization, technology, strategy, and people—where a process view is used as common framework for considering these dimensions. The approach can be graphically depicted by a modification of 'Leavitt's diamond'.

Business strategy is the primary driver of BPR initiatives and the other dimensions are governed by strategy's encompassing role. The organization dimension reflects the structural elements of the company, such as hierarchical levels, the composition of organizational units, and the distribution of work between them. Technology is concerned with the use of computer systems and other forms of communication technology in the business. In BPR, information technology is generally considered as playing *a* role as enabler of new forms of organizing and collaborating, rather than supporting existing business functions. The people/human resources dimension deals with aspects such as education, training, motivation and reward systems. The concept of business processes—interrelated activities aiming at creating a value added output to a customer—is the basic underlying idea of BPR. These processes are characterized by a number of attributes: Process ownership, customer focus, value adding, and cross-functionality.

The Role of Information Technology

Information technology (IT) has historically played an important role in the re-engineering concept. It is considered by some as a major enabler for new forms of working and collaborating within an organization and across organizational borders.

Early BPR literature identified several so-called *disruptive technologies* that were supposed to challenge traditional wisdom about how work should vbe performed.

- Shared databases, making information available at many places
- Expert systems, allowing generalists to perform specialist tasks
- Telecommunication networks, allowing organizations to be centralized and decentralized at the same time
- Decision-support tools, allowing decision-making to bc a part of everybody's job
- Wireless data communication and portable computers, allowing field personnel to work office independent
- Interactive videodisk, to get in immediate contact with potential buyers
- Automatic identification and tracking, allowing things to tell where they are, instead of requiring to be found
- High performance computing, allowing on-the-fly planning and revisioning

In the mid 1990s, especially workflow management systems were considered as a significant contributor to improved process efficiency. Also ERP (Enterprise Resource Planning) vendors, such as SAP, JD Edwards, Oracle, PeopleSoft, positioned their solutions as vehicles for business process redesign and improvement.

Methodology

Although the labels and steps differ slightly, the early methodologies that were rooted in IT-centric BPR solutions share many of the same basic principles and elements. The following outline is one such model, based on the PRLC (Process Reengineering Life Cycle) approach developed by Guha.

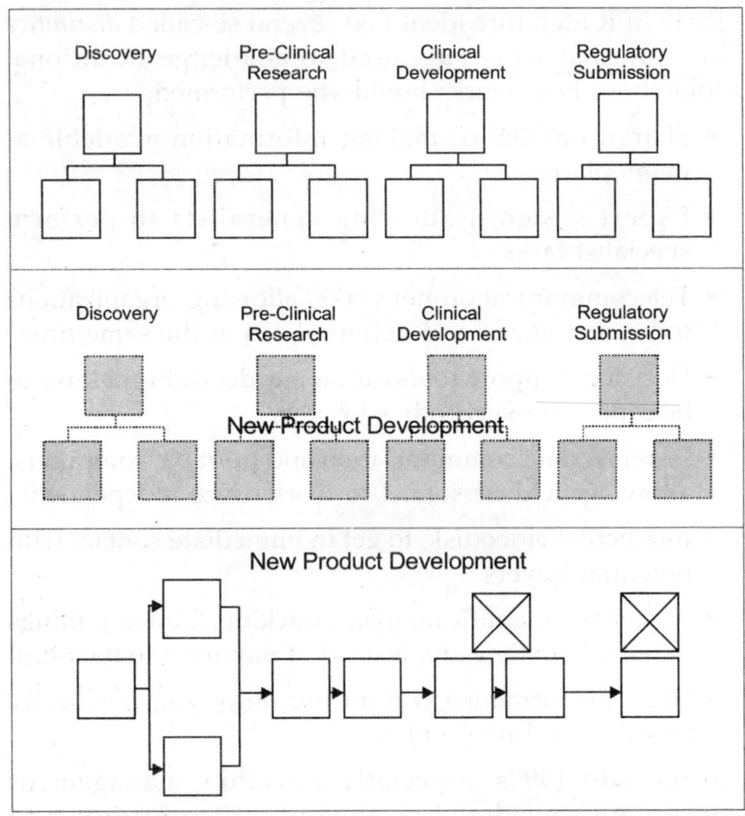

Simplified schematic outline of using a business process approach, examplified for pharmceutical R&D:

1. Structural organization with functional units
2. Introduction of New Product Development as cross-functional process
3. Re-structuring and streamlining activities, removal of non-value adding tasks

Benefiting from lessons learned from the early adopters, some BPR practitioners advocated a change in emphasis to a customer-centric, as opposed to an IT-centric, methodology. One such methodology, that also incorporated a Risk and

Impact Assessment to account for the impact that BPR can have on jobs and operations, was described by Lon Roberts (1994). Roberts also stressed the use of change management tools to proactively address resistance to change—a factor linked to the demise of many re-engineering initiatives that looked good on the drawing board.

Some items to use on a process analysis checklist are: Reduce handoffs, Centralize data, Reduce delays, Free resources faster, Combine similar activities. Also within the management consulting industry, a significant number of methodological approaches have been developed.

Successes

BPR, if implemented properly, can give huge returns. BPR has helped giants like Procter and Gamble Corporation and General Motors Corporation succeed after financial drawbacks due to competition. It helped American Airlines somewhat get back on track from the bad debt that is currently haunting their business practice. BPR is about the proper method of implementation.

General Motors Corporation

General Motors Corporation implemented a 3-year plan to consolidate their multiple desktop systems into one. It is known internally as 'Consistent Office Environment' (Booker, 1994). This reengineering process involved replacing the numerous brands of desktop systems, network operating systems and application development tools into a more manageable number of vendors and technology platforms. According to Donald G. Hedeen, director of desktops and deployment at GM and manager of the upgrade programme, he says that the process "lays the foundation for the implementation of a common business communication strategy across General Motors." Lotus Development Corporation and Hewlett-Packard Development Company, formerly Compaq Computer

Corporation, received the single largest non-government sales ever from General Motors Corporation. GM also planned to use Novell NetWare as a security client, Microsoft Office and Hewlett-Packard printers. According to Donald G. Hedeen, this saved GM 10 per cent to 25 per cent on support costs, 3 per cent to 5 per cent on hardware, 40 per cent to 60 per cent on software licensing fees, and increased efficiency by overcoming incompatibility issues by using just one platform across the entire company.

DELL Incorporated

Michael Dell is the founder and CEO of DELL Incorporated, which has been in business since 1983 and has been the world's fastest growing major PC Company. Michael Dell's idea of a successful business is to keep the smallest inventory possible by having a direct link with the manufacturer. When a customer places an order, the custom parts requested by the customer are automatically sent to the manufacturer for shipment. This reduces the cost for inventory tracking and massive warehouse maintenance. Dell's website is noted for bringing in nearly "$10 million each day in sales."(Smith, 1999). Michael Dell mentions:

"If you have a good strategy with sound economics, the real challenge is to get people excited about what you're doing. A lot of businesses get off track because they don't communicate an excitement about being part of a winning team that can achieve big goals. If a company can't motivate its people and it doesn't have a clear compass, it will drift."

Dell's stocks have been ranked as the top stock for the decade of the 1990s, when it had a return of 57,282 per cent (Knestout and Ramage, 1999). Michael Dell is now concentrating more on customer service than selling computers since the PC market price has pretty much equalized. Michael Dell notes:

"The new frontier in our industry is service, which is a much greater differentiator when price has been equalized. In our industry, there's been a pretty huge gap between what customers want in service and what they can get, so they've come to expect mediocre service. We may be the best in this area, but we can still improve quite a bit—in the quality of the product, the availability of parts, service and delivery time."

Michael Dell understands the concept of BPR and really recognizes where and when to reengineer his business.

Ford Motor Company

Ford re-engineered their business and manufacturing process from just manufacturing cars to manufacturing quality cars, where the number one goal is quality. This helped Ford save millions on recalls and warranty repairs. Ford has accomplished this goal by incorporating barcodes on all their parts and scanners to scan for any missing parts in a completed car coming off of the assembly line. This helped them guarantee a safe and quality car. They have also implemented Voice-over-IP (VoIP) to reduce the cost of having meetings between the branches.

Procter and Gamble Corporation

A multi-billion dollar corporation like Procter and Gamble Corporation, which carries 300 brands and growing really has a strong grasp in re-engineering. Procter and Gamble Corporation's chief technology officer, G. Gil Cloyd, explains how a company which carries multiple brands has to contend with the "classic innovator's dilemma—most innovations fail, but companies that don't innovate die. His solution, innovating innovation..." (Teresko, 2004). Cloyd has helped a company like Procter and Gamble grow to $5.1 billion by the fiscal year of 2004. According to Cloyd's scorecard, he was able to raise the volume by 17 per cent, the organic volume by 10 per cent, sales are at $51.4 billion up by 19 per cent, with organic sales up 8 per cent, earnings are at $6.5 billion up 25 per cent and share earnings up 25 per cent. Procter and Gamble also has a free cash flow of $7.3 billion or 113 per cent of earnings, dividends up 13 per cent annually with a total shareholder return of 24 per cent. Cloyd states: "The challenge we face is the competitive need for a very rapid pace of innovation. In the consumer products world, we estimate that the required pace of innovation has double in the last three years. Digital technology is very important in helping us to learn faster." G. Gil Cloyd also predicts, in the near future, "as much as 90 per cent of P&G's R&D will be done in a virtual world with the remainder being physical validation of results and options."

Critique

Reengineering has earned a bad reputation because such projects have often resulted in massive layoffs. This reputation is not altogether unwarranted, since companies have often downsized under the banner of reengineering. Further, re-engineering has not always lived up to its expectations. The main reasons seem to be that:

- Re-engineering assumes that the factor that limits an organization's performance is the ineffectiveness of its processes (which may or may not be true) and offers no means of validating that assumption.
- Re-engineering assumes the need to start the process of performance improvement with a "clean slate," i.e. totally disregard the *status quo*.
- According to Eliyahu M. Goldratt (and his Theory of Constraints) reengineering does not provide an effective way to focus improvement efforts on the organization's constraint.

There was considerable hype surrounding the introduction of *Re-engineering the Corporation* (partially due to the fact that the authors of the book reportedly bought numbers of copies to promote it to the top of bestseller lists).

"When I wrote about "business process redesign" in 1990, I explicitly said that using it for cost reduction alone was not a sensible goal. And consultants Michael Hammer and James Ghampy, the two names most closely associated with re-engineering, have insisted all along that layoffs shouldn't be the point. But the fact is, once out of the bottle, the re-engineering genie quickly turned ugly."

Michael Hammer similarly admitted that:

> "I wasn't smart enough about that. I was reflecting my engineering background and was insufficient appreciative of the human dimension. I've learned that's critical."

Other criticism brought forward against the BPR concept include :

- It never changed management thinking, actually the largest causes of failure in an organisation
- lack of management support for the initiative and thus poor acceptance in the organization.
- exaggerated expectations regarding the potential benefits from a BPR initiative and consequently failure to achieve the expected results.
- underestimation of the resistance to change within the organization.
- implementation of generic so-called best-practice processes that do not fit specific company needs.
- overtrust in technology solutions.
- performing BPR as a one-off project with limited strategy alignment and long-term perspective.
- poor project management.

Index